[illegible]-91

Bill

I've done a lot of writing
over past 40 years
This is my FIRST book.

I feel very Thankful for
opportunity to meet & know
you & now Love
you as a personal friend.
Thank you for all you do
to help T.P.A. Together
will impact lives of more
millions —

Your friend
Paul J

I INHERITED A FORTUNE!

PAUL J. MEYER

I INHERITED A FORTUNE!

THE SUMMIT PUBLISHING GROUP
ARLINGTON, TEXAS

THE SUMMIT PUBLISHING GROUP
One Arlington Centre, 1112 East Copeland Road, Fifth Floor
Arlington, Texas 76011
summit@dfw.net
www.summitbooks.com

01 00 99 98 97 010 5 4 3 2 1

Library of Congress Cataloging-in-Publication Data

Meyer, Paul J.
I inherited a fortune! / Paul J. Meyer
p. cm.
A collection of excerpts from the journals of Paul J. Meyer.
ISBN 1-56530-243-5
l. Meyer, Paul J. 2. Millionaires—United States—Biography. 3. Success in business.
I. Title.
HC102.5.M464A3 1997
338'.04'092—dc21

97-4570
CIP

Book Design by Mark McGarry
Composed by Texas Type & Book Works

Cover design by Dennis Davidson

Printed in the United States of America.

Notice: I have attempted to interpret and report information correctly for each story. If I have inadvertently omitted or inaccurately used any information in a story, please inform me in writing so I can correct it at next printing.

Poems were used by permission of the publisher or exhaustive efforts failed to determine the original source.

Pictures were either taken from the private collection of Paul J. Meyer or used by permission.

Illustrations by Vern Herschberger.

For information, write
Paul J. Meyer
P. O. Box 7411
Waco, TX 76714-7411
U.S.A.
or
fax 817-776-0832
(Note: This 817 area code will change to 254 on May 25, 1997.)

TO MY PARENTS

AUGUST CARL MEYER, 1892–1963

&

ISABELLE RUTHERFORD MEYER, 1892–1969

From them I inherited a fortune
of inestimable riches in attitude and philosophy
for living that have enabled me to share
my fortune with others.

"Am I going to have to do manual labor all my life?" I remember asking my mother this heartfelt question... Her response profoundly influenced the direction of my life. At that moment I knew the world's abundance was mine to earn and to possess... The choice was mine, and everything depended on my attitude.

CONTENTS

Preface *xi*
Foreword *xiii*
1 I Inherited a Fortune! 1
2 Thank You, Mrs. McCormack 7
3 After School with Mom 13
4 Junkyard Living 18
5 My Father's Magnet 25
6 The Greatest Lesson I Learned from My Mother 35
7 A Lifelong Habit: Good Nutrition and Physical Fitness 41
8 An Early Dream Fulfilled 46
9 Lessons from a Magnifying Glass 50
10 My Early Struggle with Anger 58
11 What I Was Doing When… 63
12 Happen-Chance Meetings 72
13 "How Do You Get Ahead Around Here?" 81

14 Notepads Everywhere! 90
15 Three Strikes—But Not Out 96
16 My Brother—My Hero 103
17 Work? Yes, I Love It! 110
18 My Love Affair with a Camera 118
19 Flying My Piper Cub 124
20 A Special Celebration 131
21 My Most Memorable Interview 134
22 Bartering for Business 142
23 I Was Fired from Every Job I Ever Had 150
24 Mr. Enthusiasm—My Friend Bill 158
25 My First… 166
26 Loving the Difference 175
27 Money Is Only an Idea 183
28 Taking Risks 188
29 Let's Make a Deal! 199
30 Maximizing My Strengths 206
31 Broken Trust 216
32 Negative Capability 224
33 The Most Amazing Person I Have Ever Known 230
34 "Big Ears" Pay Off 240
35 My Favorite Things 245
36 Knowledge Is Power 248
37 School of Hard Knocks 256

PREFACE

THE CONCEPT FOR THIS BOOK came from our Japanese General Director, Hei Arita. At a recent meeting of our company leaders from more than sixty countries in which we market our programs, Arita made the statement that people frequently say something like this: "*We know about the programs Paul J. Meyer writes. They have helped us set and achieve personal goals, and they have helped increase productivity in our companies. But we would like to know more about him. Would you please ask Paul J. Meyer if he keeps a personal journal or diary . . . and would he share about his parents' background, his childhood experiences, and his young adult experiences that helped form and shape the great attitude he has? Would you also ask Paul J. Meyer to tell us something about his successes and failures in other areas of life?*"

With Hei Arita's encouragement to do so, I began sharing some of the requested information from my journals, and he published this information as articles in one of his company newsletters. Some articles were also published in newspapers and periodicals throughout Asia and the Far East and Europe. These *Notes from My Journal*, as they were titled, enjoyed immense popularity, and interest increased in their being put in a book, along with additional articles. That was the beginning of this book, *I Inherited a Fortune!*

PAUL J. MEYER
FEBRUARY 14, 1997

FOREWORD

I Inherited a Fortune! is a book about attitude—the power of possessing a compelling, positive attitude of abundance. A collection of excerpts from the journals of pre-eminent businessman and tireless entrepreneur Paul J. Meyer, this book reveals a rare glimpse into the making of an extraordinarily successful individual. *I Inherited a Fortune!* is a book for all of us who long for a cool drink of water to refresh us from the relentless winds of cynicism and pessimism prevalent in so much of what we hear, read, and see today.

A wonderful title for a wonderful book—*I Inherited a Fortune!* Uncovering the gifts of life we all are entitled to, the selections in this book show us that, like Paul J. Meyer, we too can lay claim to a fortune. "As a man thinketh in his heart, so is he," says a wise ancient writer. In Paul J. Meyer's journals, the successful thoughts of a successful person speak powerfully. You will find that this stirring, heartwarming collection of memoirs puts you in touch with strengths you may have forgotten, with wisdom that may have faltered, and with hopes that may have faded.

Although he is a millionaire many times over, the inheritance Paul J. Meyer refers to is definitely not money. His parents did not have much of that to give him. What they did have, however, they generously gave: an appreciation for the blessings of life, the work ethic to employ his talents diligently, and an unshakable faith in the goodness of his Creator.

Possessing an entrepreneurial "Midas touch," Paul J. Meyer literally starts and acquires businesses in almost every arena of life he touches. After an impressive, successful insurance career, he took what he learned as a manager and motivator of others and began a corporation dedicated to "motivating people to their full potential."® That flagship company has grown into several organizations worldwide that have exceeded a total of over one billion dollars in combined sales. Other areas of interest have also developed into businesses owned by Paul J. Meyer and his family: publishing, education, printing, finance, exotic game, antique cars, auto racing, aviation, manufacturing, real estate, and much more. His entrepreneurial expertise has propelled him and his family to investments in numerous companies and ownership of more than forty corporations throughout the world.

As Paul's friend throughout more than forty years of his career, I have observed that the greatest contributing factor to his long-standing success is his *attitude*. His positive attitude, combined with his success habits and infinite thirst for knowledge, sets him apart from the typical businessperson. These traits have not only sustained him through the dramatic ups and downs frequently characterizing the risks and rewards of business ownership, but they have also catapulted him to phenomenal success.

FOREWORD

Paul J. Meyer's philosophy and attitudes run deep and wide. The rewards earned by his achievements have been used by Meyer to provide more of the true abundance of life. Accepting the abundance—and responsibilities—of life is the unique attitude reflected in these selections from Paul's journals. He views the riches of life as a trust and himself as the trustee. The beneficiaries of his inheritance are those who have used his writings to find purpose and success in their own lives. In addition, countless beneficiaries include individuals helped by one of the five foundations he and his family have established.

As you read, you will recognize that Paul's uniquely positive view of the world around him was instilled not only by his parents, but also—and this is important—by his reinforcement of his positive world view through his own deep personal commitment to this way of thinking. By his conscious choice to feed his mind diligently and carefully with only the richest, most positive ideas available, he has created his own fortune, which he generously shares with all who know him personally, through his writings or because of his various philanthropies.

You can glean from this treasure book immensely valuable seeds of success. Plant these seeds in your own mind and soul as you read these excerpts from Paul's journals, and you will reap the happiness and success your Creator has designed you for when you seek it and work for it. Begin to renew your belief, your positive attitudes, and your faith by receiving and enjoying the inheritance Paul J. Meyer so freely shares.

Dr. W.M. "Bill" Hinson, President
Haggai Institute of Advanced Leadership Training
Atlanta, Georgia
January 1, 1997

I

I INHERITED A FORTUNE!

IF MY BROTHER, sister, and I were economically poor growing up, we did not know it. Reflecting on my early years, I recognize the fact that our family did not have great wealth or many material possessions. But my parents gave me something far more valuable than "things."

As a youngster, I rode my bike seven miles into town—San Jose, California—to buy some powdered milk, day-old bread, and a few other items my mother needed. When we had the money, we bought fresh milk and fresh bread at a grocery store not far from our home. At other times I made the seven-mile ride into town where I could buy what we needed at a discount. For my magazine sales, I had outfitted my bike with a basket in the front and two side baskets.

On one particular trip my mother had told me that if I had any money left I could buy a watermelon, which I did. I loaded my purchases into my bike basket and headed home. I remember that bike ride home as if it were yesterday. The sun was shining, the wind was just right, the blue sky sparkled above me, spring flowers were everywhere, the birds were singing—the world was my cornucopia! Whistling exuberantly, I felt happy from the top of my head to the tips of my toes—and just a little "uppity." I saw people in their yards and on their porches—and all the while I was wishing they could be happy and rich like me!

I reveled in the fortune I had inherited—a fortune providing me abundance beyond my wildest expectation. I had inherited the riches of the entire creation. I remember that once, much earlier, when I was thinking about all the beauty around me, I asked my mother, "Who owns all of these things…the birds, the flowers, and the trees?"

"You own them if you are wise enough to enjoy them," she answered. I said, "How about the stars in the sky?" She said, "You own the stars, too, if you choose to." So I thought to myself, "I'll just own them. Then I'll have something to share with others that will never be used up." My mother planted the belief in me that the riches of all creation belonged to me if I wanted them and claimed them.

> My inheritance came with no restrictions or limitations.

On that seven-mile bike ride into town that day, and on many other occasions since then, I reaffirmed my belief in the fortune my parents gave me that exceeds money, houses, and lands. Since my childhood I have nourished that seed of truth, and it has flourished. I hold the power to claim a magnificent inheritance: It all depends on me—the way I choose to look at life, the way I think, and the way I act. On my numerous bike rides I never saw any signs that said "Posted. Keep Out!" or "Private. No Trespassing." Nothing restricted my enjoyment of the beauty of creation. That beauty belongs to anyone who appreciates it and claims it!

Years ago I read a book entitled *Papillon*. I identified with the main character instantly because I realized that he was a very rich person even though he spent seven years in solitary confinement. Although Papillon lived a life different from mine, in a different place, in a different time, he and I were both rich because we used our imaginations and our skills to visualize, to "act as if," and to remember those often-heard lines:

Stone walls do not a prison make
Nor iron bars a cage.

Every day Papillon took a mental trip. One day he would go shopping in Paris. Another day he might sail a schooner, gliding through the crystal blue waters of the Caribbean. Another day he would climb a mountain. Papillon's entire formula for sustaining himself and staying alive focused on affirming to himself that the whole world was his just for the taking, just for the believing, just by visualizing. He knew that if he assumed he would get nothing, he would get nothing. Approaching life with such a negative attitude would, he knew, cause him to fall into despair and oblivion, and finally, to die. He knew he would get from life exactly what he expected. So he chose to dream marvelous, magnificent dreams—and he ultimately transformed them into reality.

Like Papillon, and the Apostle Paul in his letter to the Philippians, I have learned to be content no matter what state I am in. I understand that Scripture to mean that—no matter where I am or what I have—I am happy, successful, and rich. Happiness has nothing to do with external or outside material conditions.

Papillon had no trouble accepting the abundance and universality of nature's bounty, and neither do I. I have always wondered why anyone would ever doubt the abundance of human potential. All people have talents, abilities, and qualities they never dreamed existed. Early in life I realized that vast fortunes exist in every person. All one has to do to "inherit" them is to claim them and to use them. Several years ago one of my sons, Larry, called to tell me he had just watched a sermon on television with a fantastic title—"God Don't Sponsor No Flops." That title, though not good grammar, is golden wisdom.

Here are some of the keys to believing in the abundance of the universe and the bountiful fortune we can all share:

My life is like an orchestra. I have been given the baton by my Creator. I have inherited notes that I can use in any combination I choose. The great masters—Mozart, Chopin, Beethoven, and Tchaikovsky—all used the same basic notes to compose beautiful music. Likewise, I can use them to make the kind of music I want—I am free to select the tune and the tempo of my life.

My life is like a painting. I have inherited all the colors of the rainbow. With only three primary colors—red, blue, and yellow—I can mix all the subtle tints and shades in the spectrum. I can choose any size brush or any design. I can mix ten gallons of paint or one million gallons of paint to create a panoramic canvas. My inheritance came with no restrictions or limitations. I can use one gallon of whitewash and one size brush and paint a monotonous monochrome, or I can paint like da Vinci or Rembrandt. The choice is mine!

My life is like the great literature of the world. I inherited twenty-six letters in the English alphabet. If I had been born in a different country with a different language, a different set would have been given to me to use for writing and speaking. The basic set of letters or characters is all that Longfellow, Kawabata, Shakespeare, or any of the other legendary authors ever used to give us great literature.

Decades ago when I started selling for the world's largest weekly premium life insurance company, I lived in a modest house trailer. Even though I had already improved my lot in life considerably, I planned even greater things. I persuaded the owner of the trailer park to allow me to make my trailer unique. All of the other trailers were parked north and south. I got permission to use two spaces and to turn my trailer east and west.

> I inherited a fortune! I can claim it in any place, at any time, and in any way I choose!

I built a little picket fence around my trailer. I had a sign painted and hung out in front of my house. The sign said "Meyer's Mansion."

That sign was a tangible, positive affirmation of what my parents had encouraged me to believe as a young boy. They instilled in me the belief that I had inherited a fortune and that I should encourage others to share in this marvelous inheritance. My fortune is far more valuable than any amount of money or material things my parents could have bequeathed to me. I have gone literally from rags to riches, but the most precious treasure I own is the heartfelt

Meyer's Mansion

satisfaction I receive from encouraging others to share in this fortune.

Time and experience have reinforced and expanded my desire to share my fortune with others. I do not *give* to *get*; I give because I have a need to *give*. I need to *share*. I am exceedingly grateful that my parents instilled in me early in my life the belief that rich rewards come to those who share the fortune they have inherited. What has happened to me was predicted centuries ago in Luke 6:38:

> Give, and gifts will be given to you; a good measure, pressed down, shaken together, and running over will be put into your hands. For with the same measure that you use, it will be measured back to you.

2

THANK YOU, MRS. McCORMACK

EACH OF US is a product of our past—people we have interacted with and choices we have made. The people who influenced my life most dramatically are my mother and father and several outstanding teachers. Mrs. McCormack was truly one of the significant, life-changing people who crossed my path.

Wanda McCormack

She was my first-, second-, and third-grade teacher at Cambrian Grammar School in Campbell, California. When I was about thirty-five years old, I had gained enough wisdom to realize how fortunate I was to have had such an outstanding teacher as Mrs. McCormack. So I wrote a letter thanking her for what she taught me.

Dear Mrs. McCormack,

THANK YOU, MRS. McCORMACK, FOR BEING AN INCREDIBLE ROLE MODEL. You were a vibrant example of excellence in attitude and actions. You had a heart for children. You loved us, and we loved you. You inspired my classmates and me to be our best because we knew you were thinking the best of us, expecting the best from us, and giving the best of yourself.

You never acted as if you felt superior to us. You never tried to outdo us, but you challenged each of us to outdo ourselves. You demonstrated the belief that to light the candle of another does not diminish one's own candle. You were gentle when you needed to be gentle. You were firm when you needed to be firm. When I think of all the heroes who have blessed my life, I instantly think of you. You took seriously the responsibility of influencing the impressionable children entrusted to you. You were a shining example. You set the standard. Of all the excellent teachers I ever had, you were the crown jewel.

As though it were only yesterday, I vividly remember one example of your imperturbable insight and wisdom. Rapt in attention and reluctant to disrupt, I stood at the chalkboard and wet my pants rather than asking permission to go the bathroom. Unruffled, you saved my pride and preserved my dignity when you said, "Paul, I appreciate your uniqueness, your free spirit, your great gusto for living. But there is one thing I want you to do just like everybody else—when you have to *go*, please go *to the bathroom*."

THANK YOU, MRS. McCORMACK, FOR BEING A MASTER TEACHER. You understood the principles of human behavior and learning, and you applied them diligently and consistently. We knew you genuinely desired to teach us, and your desire and enthusiasm were contagious. You knew the most effective way to teach concepts is through multisensory experiences, experimentation, and active involvement.

You applied the greatest principle of education: that great teachers are also learners. You never tried to pass yourself off as a know-it-all. You opened yourself to learning. You made learning fun! You orchestrated learning experiences that incorporated all of the senses: seeing, feeling, hearing, talking, and *doing*. When you taught us math, you used different fruits and nuts. When you taught us about Native Americans, we made costumes, we learned Native American dances, and we made a Native American village. When you introduced us to the Knights of the Round Table, we made helmets and other parts of the costume, and we acted out what was known about these knights and their gallantry. When we studied geology, you took us to Lone Hill so we could walk around the top of it and explore its possible volcanic composition and other facets of geology.

When you taught us about the stars, we studied printed material and looked at a vast collection of intriguing pictures. But we did more. We went to the observatory at Mount Hamilton. We looked through the giant telescopes. You told us what to look for at night—the Big Dipper, the Little Dipper, and the other planets in our solar system—and we shared the next day the discoveries we had made.

Most of all you encouraged us to reach for the stars. You helped us formulate action steps required to reach those stars. You taught us a can-do attitude, responsibility for our actions, and a belief that we can change the future by changing our attitudes and our actions. You were truly a master teacher!

THANK YOU, MRS. McCORMACK, FOR INSTILLING IN US A LOVE FOR LEARNING. Your commitment to being the *very best teacher* you could possibly be was equaled by your commitment to help us be the very best *learners* we could possibly be. You did not try to pour knowledge into our heads. You taught us *how to think* and *how to learn*. You helped us see the rich rewards of learning and instilled in each of us a love for learning.

You never hesitated to admit, "I don't know." But in the same breath, you would say, "Let's go to the library and find out." We learned how to use the library to find out anything we wanted to know. You also taught us that it is okay to say, "I don't know."

You set the stage for us to become active learners, and you taught us to accept responsibility for our own learning. By the time I completed the third grade, I knew the thrill and deep satisfaction that learning and using my potential provided. I began accepting responsibility for my own future.

All my life people have called me lucky. Little did they know that my luck stemmed from something I had learned long ago from you. You convinced me that chance favors the prepared mind and that luck is what happens when *preparation* meets *opportunity*. Thank you, Mrs. McCormack, for teaching me this great truth.

THANK YOU, MRS. McCORMACK, FOR SHOWING US THE VALUE OF LOVING AND ENCOURAGING EACH OTHER. Treating each other with respect in your classroom was not expected—it was required. You also taught us respect for adults and obedience to those in authority. Yours was not a grim, stern expectation; you demonstrated by your own behavior the joy and happiness resulting from loving and encouraging other people.

You also taught us the value of teamwork and sharing. You taught us that we can usually accomplish more by cooperating with each other than if all of us go our own ways. You also helped us recognize the importance of always doing our part, never shirking our duty or responsibility to others.

THANK YOU, MRS. McCORMACK, FOR BELIEVING IN THE UNIQUE POTENTIAL OF EVERY INDIVIDUAL. Your actions and words clearly demonstrated that you unequivocally believed in us. You taught us that each person possesses unique strengths and unlimited potential. You encouraged us to set challenging but realistic goals. You taught us to take appropriate action to diminish our weaknesses or compensate for them in constructive ways. But you did not spend much time on weaknesses. You were too busy helping us to maximize our strengths.

Your encouragement to me to be myself, not to conform, not to be a rubber stamp of someone else, is still a strong force in my life. Your belief in the wealth of potential in every individual is reflected in the slogan I chose for my first company: "Motivating people to their full potential."®

THANK YOU, MRS. McCORMACK, FOR SHOWING ME THE POWER OF CREATIVITY, IMAGINATION, AND VISUALIZATION. You were a *nontraditional person*, and you were a *nontraditional teacher*. You did not fit the stereotype of a teacher. You actually rode horses and even played polo expertly. You loved life and embraced it exuberantly. You inspired me to see possibilities others cannot see—to live outside the square. You taught me not merely to follow wherever the path may lead but to go, instead, where there is no path, leaving a new trail.

Because the Great Depression was gripping the nation during my first three years of school, money was scarce. But good ideas were bountiful. You taught us to consider what we *could* do, not what we *could not* do. We shared fruits from our orchard with our neighbors. We made gifts of wildflowers. Oh, how special you made me feel when I gave you a bouquet of wildflowers!

You also taught us how to write messages to create our own greeting cards. You introduced us to the joy of investing ourselves—our time and effort—by sending handwritten notes and hand-crafted gifts. Your teaching added new meaning to a line by American philosopher and writer Ralph Waldo Emerson: "The only gift is a portion of thyself."

THANK YOU, MRS. McCORMACK, FOR HELPING US RECOGNIZE THE REWARDS OF DISCIPLINE. The roots of my ability to recognize the rewards of discipline in one's life started with my parents' early emphasis on order and organization. You reinforced and strengthened my understanding of discipline. You helped form in me a lifelong philosophy I later captured in these words: "Whatever you vividly imagine, ardently desire, sincerely believe, and enthusiastically act upon must inevitably come to pass!"

Mrs. McCormack, please accept my apology for the length of this letter, but I know I speak for all your students. You changed the lives of hundreds and hundreds of your students. But your influence does not stop there. Those hundreds and hundreds of lives are now changing the lives of their children and hundreds and hundreds of others.

When Mrs. McCormack died, the minister used my letter as the eulogy. Her husband believed it best described the Total Person Mrs. McCormack was. Since I wrote that letter more than thirty years ago, I have continued to keep in touch with my other teachers and classmates. Again, speaking for them all, we collectively say, THANK YOU, MRS. McCORMACK!

3

AFTER SCHOOL WITH MOM

WE LIVED TWO MILES from the high school in Campbell, California, and I rode my bicycle to school. Whenever I had any change, I stopped on my way home to buy some Oreo cookies. I always appreciated the fact that when I got home my mother stopped what she was doing (washing clothes, ironing, cleaning the house, cooking, sewing—all the things that moms do to make a house a home) to spend some special time with each of her children. (Later she told me that some of the favorite times in her life were the times she spent with each of her three children after school.)

My usual afternoon snack, believe it or not, was *not* Oreo cookies but rather French sourdough bread and sliced white onions with butter. I have no idea of the nutritional content, but I can still remember the delectable taste in my mouth.

I went to a public school, but at the same time I feel as though I were, in today's nomenclature, "homeschooled." My mother made a special project of affirming—and reaffirming—

the positives in life by frequently asking me the question, "Did they tell you about anything in school today that you couldn't do, or that couldn't be done?" Sometimes I would report a teacher's saying something like, "You have to be in a certain place to do this or that," or "You have to have a certain education to do this or that." To these limiting comments, my mother would say, "Just remember that if there's anything you want to do, the only limitations there will ever be are the ones you place in your own mind. Where you are and what you are will always be because of the dominating thoughts that occupy your mind."

> My mother taught me that the space I occupy in life is determined by my mental attitude—no more and no less.

My mother's objective in spending time with her children was to listen to us and, at the same time, teach us principles and values. I like the way she did it. For example, when she visited people in our neighborhood who were sick, she took me with her. That was her way of teaching me to be concerned for other people. After returning home, we would talk about our experience—how we felt about it, how it encouraged others, and what else we might do to help certain people.

As we talked about school, we discussed what the teacher said. I asked questions, and my mother not only answered my questions, she amplified and expanded upon them. Because she was a former schoolteacher herself, Mother knew how to ask thought-provoking questions and to maximize my learning.

One topic my mother talked about often that I thought was particularly interesting had to do with *attitudes*—my attitude toward teachers and my attitude toward other students, including their behavior and their attitudes toward me. She asked me probing questions to explore my instincts. I guess she was checking to determine what I was thinking and how my attitudes were developing. She wanted to determine where I was in my development and to teach me how to relate constructively to all different types of personalities.

On one occasion I remember that a group of boys asked me to ride bikes with them seven miles into San Jose to go to a movie. Prior to going to the movie, however, they decided to steal something at the nickel-and-dime store. I would not go in with them, so they said some unkind things to me and left me outside the store. When they came out of the store, they wanted to put what they had stolen into the saddlebags on my bicycle. Because I refused, we got into a fight. They told me I would not be their friend anymore, and they left me alone in front of the store. I was very hurt, but I noticed that the police caught them within a block from the store. I rode home alone and, of course, shared this incident with my mother. Although I did not thank her at the time, years later I expressed my gratitude to her that she had instilled in me the right values so that when the time came for me to make a choice between

Times spent together after school were favorite times for my sister Elizabeth, my mother, me, and my brother Carl (not pictured).

right and wrong, I did not have to think about it. I knew automatically what my decision was.

I respected my mother for many reasons but especially because she encouraged all her children to be individuals. In addition, I do not remember her criticizing us one single time. She patiently trained us, coached us, and taught us, spending whatever time we needed to be with her, *one-on-one*. She was my brother's friend, *one-on-one*. She was my sister's friend, *one-on-one*. And she was my friend, *one-on-one*. Amazingly, she was also a friend of all of my sister's girlfriends. In fact, when Elizabeth's friends planned an outing or a trip, they most often wanted to take our mother with them. Our mother was a friend of all our neighbors. Whenever they had problems, they talked to my mother about them. She was a good listener and helped them think through the best solutions to their problems.

I used to assume that everybody had a mother like mine and that every grandmother was like my mother. As I grew into adulthood, I began to realize how far that was from being true. I realized also that I was one of the most fortunate people in the world!

I remember a lesson my mother taught me about money. I wanted desperately to buy a bicycle I had seen in the window of a bike shop in San Jose. I used every bit of salesmanship and persuasion I could muster to convince her she needed to loan me the money because the bike would probably be gone if I did not buy it soon. I also told her I would earn the money and pay her back. The bike was a special Schwinn racing bike, and I looked at it at least once a week in the window. It was an expensive bike—eighty-five dollars over fifty years ago—which, I suppose in today's currency, would be comparable to fifteen hundred to two thousand dollars.

My mother told me she would give me ten dollars to pay down on the bicycle. It was up to me to see if I could convince the owner that I was going to be able to borrow half of the money from my mother and then earn the other half over the summer and pay him the balance. And that is what happened! I paid back the loan from my mother by earning money buying, repairing, and selling bikes, from my magazine route, and from doing work on farms and ranches. I enjoyed the work and was highly motivated. I knew what the end result and benefit was: my Schwinn racing bike, my absolute pride and joy!

Another special after-school memory with my mother involved her assisting me in my younger years—from about seven to fourteen—to hand-make birthday cards for our friends, as well as Christmas cards and Valentine cards. My mother would buy art paper, and we would sit at the kitchen table and design, cut, paste, write, print, and draw. We would take time out only for a bite of an Oreo cookie and a little milk now and then. Those were great times!

In my catalog of memories, in my diary, and in my heart is a treasured place for my time *after school with Mom.*

4

JUNKYARD LIVING

"Make do, or do without."

"Do what you have to do, when you have to do it, with what you have to do it with."

"Necessity is the mother of invention."

SAYINGS LIKE THESE capture the attitude of my family toward dealing with the scarcity of money in the United States during the Great Depression of the early thirties. My parents were pre-eminent examples of resourcefulness. How they accepted responsibility for their lives and took the initiative to "make something out of nothing" taught me that you can live an abundant life with or without the tangible traditional wealth most societies consider important. What my parents taught me was far more valuable than all the riches and material wealth enjoyed by relatively few people at that time.

One lesson on resourcefulness I vividly remember had to do with my first bicycle. I told my parents I wanted a bike more than anything else. During those hard-pressed times there were scarcely any bikes being built. Even if there were, we had no money to buy one. My dad suggested we go to the junkyard to get an old discarded bike and rebuild it. We did just that! One of the greatest pleasures I recall enjoying with my dad was he and I working on the bike together.

Little did I realize at that time this project would launch me into buying old bikes, repairing them, and selling them. I put a sign out on the major road near our home that said "Paul's Bike Shop." People brought their bikes in the daytime while I was in school, and my mother took them in. I repaired them at night. I bought and sold over three hundred bicycles from the time I was thirteen until I was sixteen. I often wonder if my dad had been able to afford to buy me a bike and had never suggested I build one, whether I would have had such an invaluable experience. I think not.

After we had rebuilt a few bikes, my dad laughed and said, "Let's do the same thing with a car." We went to the junkyard and found a wrecked automobile—a sedan. We cut off the top except for the windshield and made a pickup truck. It had no

From a wrecked sedan, my dad and I built a serviceable pickup. Not bad looking for a "junkyard" truck, is it?

doors. Whatever pieces we lacked and could not find or buy, we made them ourselves.

These early experiences with building bikes and a pickup laid the foundation for my lifelong, invincible attitude of finding a way—or making one.

On another occasion, when winter was coming, we had nothing to provide heat for our home. On a visit to the junkyard, we found an old stove. The grate had completely burned out of it. Thinking it had no value, someone had taken it to the dump. We found a piece of steel and fashioned a grate out of it by boring holes in it with a steel drill. Then we put it in the bottom of the stove. We did not burn wood like everyone else—we burned apricot pits. We used apricot pits because the farmers gave away apricot pits just to get them carried off their farms. Firewood cost precious dollars. We also burned apricot pits because they generate more heat than wood. They were so hot that they would burn through the grate in two winters. We simply got another piece of steel and replaced the grate rather than throwing away the entire stove. This experience taught me to relate the normally unrelated and to see potential and possibilities many people never see.

A similar situation involved a barbecue grill, something my dad wanted very badly. So we went to the junkyard, which was down by a creek. We found a grate that we used for the grill. We hauled rocks from the creek to complete our barbecue grill.

Another time I can remember my dad telling me that we needed to build a fence. He asked, "How would you build a fence if you had no money or no materials?" I laughed and replied, "I guess I would go to the junkyard and find something." So again, off to the junkyard! There we found a large number of bedposts that I suppose had been discarded by some bed company. They were just the right length—about six feet. We planned to build a four-foot fence, so that would leave two feet to put into the ground. These bedposts made excellent fence posts. We mixed our own concrete. I acquired some wire for the top strand of the fence by going to a nearby turkey farm and asking if they had any extra wire they were not using. I also went to a chicken farm and asked the same question.

That junkyard fence stood for more than fifty years. When it was taken down, it was not because it was worn out but to make way for some condominiums being built on that property. Our total monetary investment in that fence was practically nothing with the exception of a sack of concrete. Even the gravel we mixed with the concrete came from the creek running alongside the junkyard.

Our work tools also came from the junkyard. We found several hammers and a hoe there with broken handles, which we repaired. We also found our rake as well as some other garden tools at the junkyard. With the new handles we put on them, they worked perfectly. We also had an incredible collection of car tools. Although they did not come directly from the junkyard, they were in a fifty-gallon drum on its way to the junkyard when the owner asked if we wanted any of them. We simply intercepted these tools before they were discarded at the junkyard.

Not only did I learn to repair tools, I learned the importance of having the right tool (in mint condition) for the job. I learned from these early days with my father and our tools that the best job is accomplished with good tools, whether the tools be hammers and wrenches, the right attitude, or specific skills, and whether the job be rebuilding a bike, a car, a stove, or a barbecue grill. I also learned how to make the leap from *pieces* to *reality*. I learned that one must have a vision and the right tools for bringing it into reality, piece-by-piece, sometimes with a plan that exists only mentally, other times with a complex written plan.

I learned as a young person that most women love flowers. So on birthdays and other occasions when I wanted to give a gift to one of the women in my young life (most of them were on my magazine route), I dug up wildflowers I saw along the road and put them into empty coffee cans. I put Christmas paper or other attractive paper around the pot and added the finishing touches with ribbon I got from my mother. I knew the ladies on my magazine route enjoyed my gifts, but I had no idea how much until the stories started coming back to me. Not only did I appreciate their comments, I was also grateful for the referrals these women gladly gave me for my magazine route.

My dad could look at trees and mentally turn them, plank-by-plank, into beautiful furniture. Similarly, he could look at an old shack and visualize using its materials for a far more handsome and useful structure. Once when a house was to be torn down with the lumber destined for the junkyard, we helped dismantle the house in exchange for the lumber. Again, we saw possibilities no one else visualized.

> I learned that few items are totally unfit for use and must be discarded or rejected. I learned that this truth also applies to people.

Numerous items we found in the junkyard were of no use to us. But my dad must have repaired at least fifty different items, such as a kerosene lamp, a clock, and various other items we traded with neighbors for items we could use. Looking back now, I realize that I learned more than just to repair junk and make it useful for someone else. I learned to help meet the needs of other people and the satisfaction that comes from helping others.

When I started Success Motivation Institute, Inc. I already knew how to *make do* or to *make a way*—either make something I needed or use an alternative—I knew how to thrive on "junk-yard living":

- When we needed file cabinets, we went to the salvage warehouse, selected the best ones, repaired them, painted them, and used them.
- We transformed used doors into desks simply by putting legs on them. They provided spacious working areas.
- Rather than using our money to buy new shipping boxes, we went to the local grocery store and asked for the empty grocery boxes. We packed and shipped everything for the first couple of years in these recycled grocery boxes.
- The salvage warehouse was also the source of other items required in our work—typewriters. We had only one typewriter in the company to begin with. John Cook, our general manager and one of the few employees in the company, told me we needed additional typewriters. At a salvage place in Dallas I bought ten typewriters for sixty-five dollars, an average cost of $6.50 apiece. When I brought them back to our office, John asked, "What are we going to do with these? They don't work—they are a bunch of junk." I replied to John, "Of course they don't work. That is why I paid only $6.50 for each one of them." In no time we had taken the working parts from the ten typewriters and ended up with six working typewriters, each with a value of about seventy-five dollars. Before John's "bunch of junk" wore out, they were used for more than five years.

Whenever we could, we "made do" with what we had—or did without. Knowing how to thrive on junkyard living also enabled us to save money and use it for areas that did not lend themselves to that approach: advertising, sales promotion, and producing quality products.

As I review my journal from long ago and reminisce, I recapture and savor the magnificent sense of accomplishment provided by taking something trashed out, bent, broken, or in other ways less than perfect and straightening it, repairing it, or in some way making something useful and attractive from it. If I had been able simply to go to the store and buy everything new, it would not have provided the same satisfaction and appreciation.

In my reminiscing I also wonder if my father knew he was teaching me more than making beauty and usefulness from junk. I wonder if he knew that his building a man from a little boy was by far the greater lesson.

5

MY FATHER'S MAGNATE

IF YOU COULD VISIT ME today in my Waco, Texas, office, you would see a glassed-in case displaying a collection of antique tools. Unusual? Yes. But if those tools could speak, they would tell some fascinating stories. These tools belonged to my father, a decisive and determined German craftsman who believed that the skillful use of the right tool for each job was essential to creating the desired masterpiece—furniture, cabinet, or any other object a craftsman fancied. My father's workmanship confirmed the validity of his belief.

My father also believed that predictable laws govern the universe. As my life experiences provide me with an increasing understanding of the laws of physics, chemistry, mathematics, and the social sciences, my agreement with this analytical man increases. My father taught me hands-on use of every one of these tools, but he also used each one to teach a principle. One tool stands out in my memory, for my father used it to demonstrate a law far more intriguing than any of the other laws governing craftsmanship or the entire universe. That fascinating tool was my father's magnet.

Only about six inches wide and four inches long, my father's magnet opened doors to understanding far beyond anything its small size and inauspicious appearance might suggest. My father showed me how to point the magnet one way to repel nails and other metal objects and then to point it the other way to attract them. Pointing the magnet's negative pole toward the metal items and making them scatter pell-mell was sheer delight to me as a young boy. Even more amazing was using the positive end to attract the metal items instantly.

Experimenting with this magnet brought the law of attraction to life for me. *Positives attract, and negatives repel.* My father emphasized that this truth not only applies to magnets and metal items, but it also applies to attitudes and actions. When we point our attitude toward positive results, the results are positive. The power of a positive attitude is far-reaching; it goes well beyond the immediate boundaries of our thought processes.

Like an invisible magnet, positive attitudes reach out and draw into our presence the results that we so intensely wish to attract.

In contrast, when people direct their mental attitudes toward negative results, they get exactly what they expect—negative consequences or nothing at all. When people allow fear, worry, doubt, indecision, and other forms of negative thinking to determine the direction of their mental attitude—and ultimately their actions—they shut off the positive power of their magnets. When they focus on the *cannots* rather than the *cans*, the outcome is predictably negative. Negative thinking always repels; it consistently produces negative consequences!

My father's magnet helped me understand a closely related success principle dealing with hard work. A lot of people appear to be working feverishly, always busy, but they never reach the goals they desire. No matter how hard they work, my father emphasized, they can never attract a successful and positive situation in life unless *they are pointed in the right direction*. Individuals must direct their attitudes and actions toward their goals, or no amount of work will ever result in achieving them. To be successful, all efforts must be lined up, consistent with, and in support of achieving the desired goals.

Similarly, for the law of attraction to work most powerfully in our lives, we must *believe in it*. As my father stressed, I first had to *believe* that the magnet possessed power. Attracting the nails had to be *mentally* accomplished before it could be *physically* accomplished. But even if I had confidence that the positive end of the magnet would attract, nothing happened simply on that belief until I took action based on my belief and pointed the positive end of the magnet toward the objects I wanted to attract.

After people set goals, they must *believe* they can reach those goals and then take action on that belief. I never give recognition to the possibility of defeat in any area of my life because I point my mental magnet toward the object of my desire and focus all of my magnetic energy on my goal. My belief, my faith, my attitude, my attention, and my actions are directed like a giant magnet toward the results I wish to attract. No science, dogma, creed, or religion in the world will let me attract anything if I have a negative mental attitude and a disbelief that it will ever happen.

Belief in the law has to be in our bone marrow, in our white corpuscles and red corpuscles, and in our skin; it must show in our eyes, be reflected in our voices, show in our walk, and be felt from the energy we generate. I live with belief in this principle. No one would ever say about me, "This man lacks confidence," or "This man has no faith in what he is doing," or "This fellow doesn't really think he can attract the positive results he is seeking."

My hobby of antique cars provides a good example. Ordinarily, no one buys them without seeing them first. But I have bought over one hundred antique cars after only talking to someone on the phone, asking questions, and seeing pictures. I trust my knowledge to know what questions to ask, and I trust my judgment. I have been disappointed only once. Since I have developed this ability to buy cars sight unseen, I decided to sell some of my cars the same way. I tried it and it worked. For example, one winter day I knew there was bad weather in the northern part of the United States. I thought to myself, "I'll get out all my leads in the north because those people are snowed in. They're nervous, because they haven't been out of the house for several days." I called a lead one Sunday afternoon in Vermont who was seventy-three years old and snowed in. I sold him an antique car—the Model A—without his ever seeing it.

"How cold is it up there?" I asked the gentleman. He answered, "Twenty-six below zero." As we began discussing the car, he said, "I'll have to come down there to see that car because I've never bought a car without seeing it first." I asked, "How many cars have you bought?" He answered, "About eighty." I said, "Well, you don't have to see this car. You can trust me." I pointed my magnet in a positive direction, and he felt the confidence he could place in me over the telephone via satellite from over two thousand miles away.

He went on to the next question. "How do you want me to pay you?" I said, "Send a cashier's check." He said, "I'll send one by Federal Express tomorrow if I can get out of my house." That was Sunday. I got the check Tuesday. I do not know how that seventy-three-year-old man got out of his snowed-in house at twenty-six below zero to send a FedEx on Monday so I would receive my check on Tuesday. But I do know I turned my belief, my positive expectancy, up to full force. And it worked.

"Look at this magnet," my father once instructed me. "It does no good unless it is put to use ... put into action." He went on to explain that a magnet sitting on a shelf, not doing what it was designed to do, is much like a complacent person whose attitude and actions whisper, "I fear taking action. I am afraid of taking a chance." In reality, such people fear reaching out for more because they do not believe they can get more. Because of their disbelief and complacency, these individuals find pseudosecurity in assuming a do-nothing position. They build a wall around their limited self-image to protect it, and they live out their days in negative expectancy. My father emphasized that his magnet was not designed to sit on a shelf doing nothing. Tools are useful only when they help create desired results. Similarly, human beings are not created for a stark, immobile, lackluster, unfulfilling existence either. My father helped me see another simple but profound principle: "People are happy and fulfilled only when they use their lives to fulfill the noble and inspiring purposes for which their Creator designed them."

My father's magnet demonstrated to me yet another important success principle. That is, the positive force and negative force of a magnet cannot coexist in the same end of the magnet. Neither can faith and fear coexist in the same mind. People full of fear, worry, doubt, indecision, and other negative thinking cannot at the same time possess faith, confidence, belief, and positive expectancy. My father and mother encouraged me to believe that success depends on rejecting all negative thoughts and attracting and filling my mind with powerful positive thoughts. I accepted then what my parents encouraged me to believe. I still believe it.

Just as the law of attraction worked with my negotiations on the antique car, it works in all other areas of life. For instance, what is the status of the health of my body? If it is not doing well and I am not achieving the goals I have for it, I need to change my thoughts and actions. When I expect strength, vigor, buoyancy, energy, capacity, and endurance from my body, the results start materializing because my thoughts motivate me to take the actions that create the positive results. Research has proven—and my own experience has validated the research—that if we persistently and constantly entertain thoughts of belief and positive expectancy, our bodies respond positively because of the constructive actions taken on the basis of positive attitudes. No thought is so small or unimportant that it fails either to *repel* or *attract*. This law is true when applied to health as well as to any other area of life.

Consider the Mental and Educational area of life, for example. Some people with high IQs or advanced educational degrees are not particularly successful because IQ or education alone is not enough to attract success, wealth, or happiness. If intellectually gifted or highly educated people dwell on fear, worry, indecision, negative thinking—such as all the reasons why something *cannot* be done—or if they dwell on the past, the results are predictable. The outcome of such an attitude is negative because people draw to themselves just what they expect. If they expect little, they get little. No mind is intelligent enough or highly educated enough to attract success unless it is bolstered by belief and positive expectancy.

As intelligent as Einstein was, for instance, his intellect alone was not powerful enough to formulate the theory of relativity without his persistent and positive confidence that he could figure it out. Einstein's positive magnet of belief and confidence gave force to actions that ultimately led to the scientific theory that made him famous.

The principle of attraction also works in the Social and Cultural area of life. I know a woman, for example, who radiates a positive attitude. When she walks into a social gathering and starts talking to people, they look up and pay attention. The love that woman has for people and the interest she demonstrates in them creates a magnetic field around her and attracts people to her. She turns on her positive magnet, and it attracts people automatically, predictably. What happens illustrates the law of attraction because people likewise love that woman and are interested in her.

Numerous examples are also seen in the power of belief in the Spiritual and Ethical area of life. I am not surprised at this because Scriptures have told us if we have faith even the size of a mustard seed, we can move mountains, and as we think in our hearts so are we. Examples of positive ethics also abound. Positive ethics consistently result in positive consequences. Taking right actions pays off as predictably as the positive end of the magnet attracting nails and other metal items.

Since those early days in my father's workshop with various tools, and especially with my father's magnet, I have seen many different functions for magnets. The varied and abundant uses of magnets remind me of one of my favorite sayings: "The world is my cornucopia!"

This is my affirmation: I live in a world of abundance.

> Just as the uses of a magnet are varied and numerous, the world is full of varied and numerous opportunities.

Not all people take advantage of opportunities because they fail to believe in a world of abundance. They possess a poverty mentality, convinced that only a limited supply of success exists and that there is not enough to go around to everyone who wants some of it. Some negative thinkers even believe we have to duel each other to get a portion of that limited supply.

In contrast, I have observed that those who have a no-limitations belief in themselves and in their Creator, a no-limitations belief in the potential of other people, and a no-limitations belief in the abundance of our world are the ones who enjoy abundance in all areas of their lives. "I'm going out to shake the money tree today," I used to announce in jest. Or I would joke about the streets being lined with whatever I visualized as desirable. The trees were producing whatever fruit I believed they were growing. They were then, and they are now. It is simply a matter of attitude.

A recent business deal serves as a good example of the power of the law of attraction, abundance, and positive expectancy. I bought four lots in the boonies for $85,000 in spite of their being offered for sale at $160,000. When I offered the owner $75,000, he said the offer was insane. Not discouraged, I replied, "Yes, but I have cash. I will give you $85,000 and can pay you today." He quickly responded, "I'll take it." So I bought the land for 55 percent of what the owner was originally asking for it. Positive expectancy helped seal the deal!

Deserts can also illustrate the law of attraction, positive expectancy, and abundancy. Every once in a while, a green oasis is found in a desert. Coachella Valley, in the Southern California desert, for example, is one of the most beautiful small valleys I have ever seen anywhere. It is about thirty miles long and ten miles wide. It was not made by forces of nature, but by the hard work of human hands. Years ago who would ever have thought this oasis possible in the midst of a sandy desert?

Certainly not an individual with a negative mentality! Someone with an abundance attitude, a positive expectancy, a magnet turned fully facing the positives, saw the possibilities in the middle of this arid desert and developed a beautiful oasis.

The lessons I learned from my father's magnet have served me well!

This oasis example, as well as many of my life experiences, convinces me that if we want plenty, we have to think plenty. If we want wealth, we have to think wealth. If we want success, we have to think success. If we want health, we have to think health. And if we want happiness, we must think happiness.

Abraham Lincoln said, "We're about as happy as we make up our minds to be." We can choose.

Turning the positive end of the magnet toward the conditions we wish to attract is essential for bringing those conditions into reality. People often call me lucky, but my achievements—wealth, success, health, and happiness—are not the results of luck. Neither are they accidental. They are the results of faith and the law of attraction. It is as simple as that.

6

THE GREATEST LESSON I LEARNED FROM MY MOTHER

FIRST, LET ME ask you some questions:

- Have you ever been discouraged? I have.
- Have you ever been down? I have.
- Have you ever been depressed? I have.
- Have you ever been hit from every direction by hurdles, obstacles, or problems in your home or in your business? I have.

If you answered "yes" to one or more of these questions, I urge you to make a list of all the negative events or circumstances you experienced in the last year. Be sure to think of everything—every downer, everything that has turned against you in business, every problem at home—every trouble in every single area of your life. Write them all down.

Next, I would like for you to ceremonially destroy or get rid of your list by tearing it up into little pieces, feeding it into a shredder, burning it, or putting it in your "forgettery."

A "forgettery" is an idea I have taught to small children. One day, we would make an imaginary "forgettery" box and then have everyone march up and put the list of all the bad things that had happened to them in the box. Then we would use our imagination to visualize burning the whole box and its contents.

The next step is really exciting. Make a list of everything you still have:

Two hands—I saw a person this week with none.

Two legs—I saw another person a couple of weeks ago with only one leg.

Two eyes—I have a dear friend who is blind. He is a miracle person because he looks at the positives in his life.

Two ears—My mother's hero was Helen Keller, who could neither see nor hear. Still, she clearly learned to concentrate on the positives in her life.

Family—I read this very morning about a man in my town who lost his family in a fire. I cannot imagine the enormous pain of that loss.

Your mind—I have a neighbor who has just developed Alzheimer's and cannot remember much of anything.

The beautiful world around you—The sky, the sun, the moon, the rain, the flowers, the myriad colors of butterflies, the birds singing, the grass. Music, poetry, good books.

Your business—The banks are still full of money. People still have plentiful savings. Ninety-eight percent of those who desire to work have jobs.

Beginning when I was very young, my mother instilled in me the belief that it was right and good always to be thankful. She taught me to face each new day as a gift, a reason for celebrating. To regain an attitude of celebration and thankfulness, ask yourself these thought-provoking questions, giving them your serious consideration:

- If this were the first day for you in your business or on your job, would you get up a little earlier than usual?
- How would you dress?
- What would you have for breakfast?
- Who would you see first?
- How positive and excited would you be as you entered the day concentrating on the positives in your life that you just listed?

When I consider these questions myself, I feel like jumping up and down with excitement. Just thinking about the *power of thoughts and attitudes* energizes me. I know the climate I create through my thoughts and attitude is the only environment I will ever live in. For many years these affirmations have helped me create my own "ecology":

- When it is pouring down rain, I choose to see the sun.
- When it is dark at night, I visualize the moon.
- When there is adversity, I develop an attitude of gratitude and list all the things I am thankful for.

As you keep your blessings in mind, you tend to increase them. According to the law of attraction, "You actually bring favorable circumstances and conditions into being by thinking about and concentrating on the positives in your life."

Marcus Aurelius long ago stated that the world we live in is created by *how we think*. If you disdain, resent, or view pessimistically your life condition, then your awareness of blessings begins to shrivel up and you believe they have become fewer in number. The opposite attitude—*concentrating on the positive*—helps create the opposite results. Life grows, blessings increase, well-being flourishes, and circumstances prosper above and beyond, exceeding our greatest expectations. I have seen this in my life and the lives of many others.

I have a friend in Waco, Texas, named John Cook. He was the first employee of my first company. When I hired John in 1960 over thirty-five years ago, he had just suffered three kinds of polio. He had dropped from six feet, four inches and 250 pounds to six feet and one hundred pounds. Amazingly, even in his iron lung he smiled and was thankful because he was alive. With a back brace and in enormous pain, he started as the general manager of our company. Anywhere John went in the company there was a magic aura:

- If people were arguing, they stopped.
- If people were thinking negatively, they started thinking positively because they observed that John never saw a negative, never heard a negative, and never believed a negative.
- If the stock market went down, John did not care.
- If there was a flood or other disaster, he encouraged the people to rise to the top and handle it. And they did.

John Cook simply took our business ups and downs in stride. The whole office was a reflection of John's grateful and positive attitude. It was almost as though he did not allow it to be any other way. He had a great synergistic effect on everybody's work.

Even with his severe physical difficulties, he was one of the most emotionally healthy people I ever knew.

An economic recession occurred in 1962, and I remember listening to John encourage the employees. I took the same powerful message to the sales force. With a compelling positive mental attitude, everyone in our company set a goal not to read the newspaper, not to watch any television, and not to listen to any gossip or negatives for thirty days but simply to go out and work. We increased production 50 percent! What I saw in John's attitudes and actions was exactly what I learned from my mother long ago: "Concentrate on the positives in your life. Start each day thinking about and reciting what you are thankful for."

In any culture or any country, it is easy to fall into the habit of dwelling on adversities. Watching television, reading the newspaper, hearing people everywhere talk about the negatives all lead you to think of the *minus* factors in your own situation instead of the *plus* factors. When you indulge in this negative mental thinking, it becomes a destructive habit. You may even reach the point where you are emotionally paralyzed, unable to handle life's daily situations—even nonthreatening, routine ones.

But you can still change! Write down everything you have to be thankful for—your physical attributes, your mental capabilities, your family—*everything*. Simply make a list of all the positive factors in your life. When you concentrate on what you have *going for you*, you create a right attitude, you snap out of worry or depression, and then you go forward!

When you *concentrate on the positives in your life*, you stir up the desire to get moving, to seize the day, to take action, to conquer every adversity that jeopardizes well-being or prosperity, to take advantage of every opportunity that comes your way, and

My mother taught me the awesome power of concentrating on the positives in life.

even to create opportunities that do not exist. *Being thankful for what you have* creates a twinkle in your eye, a spring in your step, and a magic sound in your voice. A thankful, positive attitude is dramatic, magnetic, and electrifying. How much more productive would you be if you adopted this attitude? How much more successful would you be?

This attitude is a gift, and it is your choice whether or not you accept it. It is a gift I chose to accept from my mother. It is *the greatest lesson I learned from her*! This lesson has provided me a magic carpet that has taken me everywhere in the world, and it has made available to me vast opportunities to help many others use more of their God-given potential.

7

A LIFELONG HABIT: GOOD NUTRITION AND PHYSICAL FITNESS

Becoming a total person and living a balanced life has been the central theme of my full-length courses and programs for more than thirty years. I have consistently emphasized setting goals in all areas of your life: Family and Home, Financial and Career, Mental and Educational, Physical and Health, Social and Cultural, and Spiritual and Ethical. People the world over are eager for this kind of information. They always ask me when I am making a speech, conducting a seminar, or just dining out, how I stay in good shape, what kinds of foods I eat, and which foods I avoid.

Early in my life I determined that taking care of this house we live in—our physical body—is each individual's responsibility. I do not remember how I knew this important truth at such a young age. Several factors may account for my early understanding. My mother was reared on a farm where fresh vegetables were always available. In addition, she served as head nurse at the Bronson Hospital in Kalamazoo, Michigan. Because of the role model her parents provided and because of her professional training as a nurse and as a teacher, my mother naturally emphasized the importance of good nutrition in our home. Another strong influence occurred when I was between the ages of fourteen and seventeen. This was during World War II, and our family had what was called a Victory Garden. My father took great pride in winning first place in Santa Clara County, California, for our Victory Garden. The wide variety of vegetables and other produce, as well as the layout and design of our Victory Garden, always earned first place. Every kind of vegetable you could imagine grew in our garden. Besides strawberries, raspberries, and blackberries, fifteen different kinds of fruit trees provided a bountiful harvest.

Learning early in my life the value of combining good nutrition and a solid exercise program has helped me continue to enjoy good health.

Another powerful incentive that reinforced my ambition to be physically fit occurred when a classmate hit me, knocking the wind out of me. I remember lying on the sidewalk crying and vowing that I would not allow that to happen again. I was blessed over the next twelve months with gaining fifty pounds in weight and nine inches in height! During all this time I had been going to the YMCA regularly to work out. The combination of eating fresh fruits and vegetables, receiving guidance from my mother on nutrition, and participating regularly in vigorous exercise enabled me to attain the physical body I so desired.

A healthy body coupled with discipline helped me to break all the physical fitness records as an eighteen-year-old in the United States Paratroopers in 1946 and 1947. Little did I realize at the time that my interest in nutrition and physical fitness had also empowered me to turn down invitations to smoke and to go out with the boys and get drunk.

I am fully convinced now that all of these influences and successes fueled my desire to write courses and to tell others about the validity and the power of becoming a Total Person.

During the last forty-five to fifty years I have nurtured the desire to take good care of myself and to stay in good shape. I have stayed true to my early commitment and determination to develop the very best fitness and nutrition habits. My regimen now is the same one I have followed for many years. Six days every week I exercise in one of these ways:

1. Walk three to four miles either by myself or with my wife, Jane—most often with Jane.
2. Ride a bicycle ten to twenty miles, or in inclement weather, ride the stationary bike for forty minutes at a brisk pace. (The stationary bike is most reliable because it is available regardless of the weather.)
3. Use a treadmill or a stair climber for approximately forty minutes.

To add interest and variety, I sometimes alternate these exercises, engaging in a different one each day of the week. My main goal is to get aerobic exercise six days a week, taking anywhere from forty minutes indoors to an hour and a half outdoors.

In the area of nutrition, I have been called a health nut because I do not drink colas or eat beef more than once a month. Instead, I enjoy a diet of fish and chicken accompanied by rice and a variety of fresh vegetables—squeezed vegetable juice, steamed vegetables, and vegetable salads all form an integral part of my diet. For breakfast I enjoy a half dozen types of rice cereal mixed together topped with fresh fruits such as raspberries, blackberries, or strawberries, as well as bananas, peaches, and nectarines. I do not put milk on my cereal—I put fresh orange juice—so I have a no-fat, healthful breakfast.

Good nutrition and physical fitness are based on respect for one's body. Our bodies are temples or homes where we live. We should take care of our bodies just as carefully as we take care of our house and other possessions. You would not abuse your home by breaking the windows, setting fire to it, filling it with unhealthy substances, or neglecting to maintain it and keep it in tip-top shape. Taking care of your home is very important, but taking care of the home where your mind and spirit live is even more important. A healthy body provides a high quality of life that enables you to be more successful in every area of life. Stay physically fit with a sound exercise program and a low-fat, nutritious diet, and you can enjoy these benefits:

Good nutrition and physical fitness are based on respect for one's body.

- Adequate stamina, strength, and endurance for all activities
- Increased ability to think clearly, to reason well, and to make wise decisions

- Vivid imagination
- Expanded creativity
- Intuition
- Strong self-image
- High level of self-confidence
- Satisfying interpersonal relationships with family, friends, business associates, and clients

A healthy body and mind form a fountainhead of desire and commitment. You simply have adequate energy to direct toward the fulfillment of your goals!

A benefit of taking good care of my body and mind that I did not necessarily plan for or anticipate is better health in later life. Close to seventy, I feel more like fifty. I cannot even imagine what retiring and not working would be like. Being inactive is simply out of the question for me. I love working, and I love being productive. I wake up in a new world every day with the wonder and excitement of a young child. I can hardly wait to get started in the morning and to seize the opportunities of the day. I love making a contribution! A lifelong dedication to taking care of my body and my mind makes all this possible.

8

AN EARLY DREAM FULFILLED

KNOWING MORE about my ancestry and what motivated various family members—especially my father—to immigrate to the United States was an early dream of mine. At this season of my life—nearly three score and ten—I have wondered, "What was my father's attitude toward leaving his loved ones and all that was familiar to travel to a strange, new world?"

As a child, I heard many stories about my father coming to the United States from Germany in his early twenties. That would have been between 1910 and 1916. At that time, his family lived in Colmar, Germany, which is now part of France.

My father left home at age eighteen and moved to Berlin. As soon as he saved sufficient funds, he bought passage on a ship to the United States. I remember hearing him tell about how the ship was lost at sea for fifty-six days. The passengers were crowded inhumanely and suffered tremendous hardships to make this journey. I have always respected those undaunted individuals determined to improve their lot in life. Their intense commitment, fearless adventuresomeness, and their willingness to lay their lives on the line still stir my deepest emotions.

When my father reached the United States, one of his first sights was the Statue of Liberty. This impressive symbol of the freedom and opportunity these hardy immigrants sought stands on an island alongside Ellis Island. The immigrants were processed on Ellis Island, which is in New York Harbor right off Manhattan.

I recently achieved part of my larger goal—that is, to go to Ellis Island and visualize and relive the steps my father took upon arriving in the United States and to imagine what it was like at that particular time in history. From 1892 to 1924 more than twelve million people—mostly from Europe—packed up their belongings and sailed to the New World. Now, some

My father joined millions of other immigrants processed through Ellis Island on a pilgrimage of hope and positive expectancy.

eighty years later, more than one hundred million Americans—over 40 percent of our country's population—can trace their ancestry to immigrants who came through the gates of Ellis Island.

It can be said quite literally of my father, that without his dream, his desire, and his determination, I would not be here. There never would have been a Paul J. Meyer, and there never would have been my first company dedicated to helping one another develop and grow and to use one's potential. So I thank God for my father's courage to walk away, so to speak, telling his parents and his three sisters good-bye, knowing he would never see them again because he would never return to his homeland. At the breakfast table as a young boy about ten years old, I heard my father telling my mother that he left his homeland because he did not agree with the thinking of the German government at that time. I have always admired my father's courage to stand up for his convictions.

The chronicles and records reveal that the processing procedure for immigrants was far from pleasant, especially for the sick, those who did not have a skill or trade, and those with other problems. All the male immigrants were required to go before a board and prove that they had a trade they could use in the United States. They also had to provide proof that someone had agreed to sponsor them and provide them a place to stay. In addition, they had to have at least twenty-five dollars with them before they were released from Ellis Island to go on their way. My father was one of the fortunate ones because he had worked hard to become a master mechanic and a master cabinetmaker. These skills helped him pass through the immigration process. My father's first job on arriving in America was working in the shipyards in Brooklyn, New York. Again, my father's example, I am sure, played a large part in forming my belief in the importance of developing one's potential to provide a needed service or product to others.

As I stood on Ellis Island in the same place my father might have stood and sat on the same benches, tears unashamedly ran down my cheeks. I was so thankful that Jane was there with me, as well as my daughter Leslie and her boyfriend and my other daughter Janna and her husband, Randy. It was deeply gratifying to me that they could see what I saw and experience what I was experiencing.

Randy and Janna took this picture of Leslie, Jane, and me when we all enjoyed a trip to New York City to visit the Statue of Liberty—a symbol of freedom and opportunity.

After a few years in New York, my father moved progressively westward, saving money so he could reach his ultimate goal of living in California. At the time he met my mother, he was a carpenter and was working for the husband of my mother's sister. My mother was a schoolteacher in Michigan and had come to California to visit her sister. One evening my father was invited to dinner while she was visiting her sister. Their meeting was another fortunate coincidence for me!

As I reflect on all the events that have shaped my life, I am struck by the fact that in this time in history we all, regardless of our home country, are the fortunate recipients of a rich heritage—the freedom to become all that we possibly can.

9

LESSONS FROM A MAGNIFYING GLASS

WHEN PEOPLE ASK my good friend of over forty years, Dr. Bill Hinson, "What is Paul Meyer's most outstanding trait or characteristic?" Bill always says, "It's Paul's ability to focus with the intensity, concentration, and commitment of a laser."

What a wonderful compliment! Do you know the power of a laser? A laser amplifies and strengthens lights and produces a thin, intense beam of light that can burn a hole in a diamond, carry the signals of many different television pictures at the same time, drill eyes in surgical needles, remove diseased body tissue in surgery, or even monitor shifts in the earth's crust. When a laser beam is concentrated on one small area, it can produce temperatures higher than 5500° Celsius. It is gratifying that Bill, a high-energy person himself, says I demonstrate the characteristics of a laser—precision, intensity, power, and focus—a truly awesome force!

I remember Bill asking me at least thirty-five years ago, "Where did you learn to focus on a job with such intensity?" I told him a story about my father's magnifying glass.

On an afternoon I will never forget, my father said he wanted to show me something. He took out his magnifying glass (it was about four inches in diameter) and held it steadily about an inch away from the fender on our old car. I was astonished at what I saw happen.

My father held a magnifying glass so that the rays of sun focused on the fender of our old car—the paint peeled right off! The magnificent magnifying glass taught me for the first time the powerful principle of focus.

My father explained, "This magnifying glass teaches an important lesson that you—and many grownups—should learn. Just like the magnifying glass focuses the light into a powerful force, your ability to focus can help you reach your goals. Focus the whole weight of your personality toward a job; give the job the full impact of your total attention and concentration."

To help make his point, my father then held my hand under the magnifying glass—until I hollered, "Ouch!" The burning heat on my hand, along with my father's words, made the lesson of the magnifying glass unforgettable. The indelible memory of that kind of energy and that kind of concentration changed my life forever. The magnificent magnifying glass demonstrated graphically the powerful principle of focus. A long time after the magnifying glass lesson, lasers were developed to concentrate a beam of light. Whether from a magnifying glass or a laser, the concentration of light and energy, when channeled correctly, produces phenomenal results!

As I began teaching others about motivation and success, I coined the phrase "wearing success blinders." When people wear success blinders, it means that they look neither to the right nor left, neither up nor down, but only straight ahead. They develop the capacity to ignore distractions. They are able to shut out the entire world of distracting sight and sound. With total focus, they are blind and unhearing to anything but the object of their desire.

The big payoff for me came in making individual sales one-on-one. I focused totally on the sales presentation with the full weight of my personality. Like a laser, I focused my presentation in a narrow beam aimed directly at my prospect. I captured all my energy and channeled it as a powerful force to help me communicate with my prospective clients. They were always overwhelmed by the attention and focus I gave them. I was fully committed to fill whatever need my prospects had, so far as my abilities would reach.

I was in my mid-twenties before I fully realized what an incredible asset this intensity and focus on success could be. When making decisions and solving business problems, I directed the complete capacity of my mind toward a single point with great intensity. When I started in the life insurance business, I worked for the nation's largest weekly insurance premium company. This company offered a variety of policies. I felt my best bet, however, would be to study their rate book and figure out which policy would fulfill the greatest need for the greatest number of prospects I had at that particular time. I memorized the rates and did not use the rate book. Ninety percent of my sales were on one special policy. I became a specialist—an expert—with this one contract. Because of my focus and specialization, I led the company and broke every record that had been previously set in that company up to that time since its founding fifty years earlier.

I followed the same plan when I worked for the largest exclusive ordinary life insurance company. I specialized on a specific market—airline pilots—and a specific policy. I had more success with those pilots than other insurance agents who were promoting a wider range of policies. Again, I was the leading producer in the company. That is the way it went throughout my insurance career … focus and specialization.

When I trained other life insurance agents, I emphasized the importance of choosing a specific market. In training sessions, one of the illustrations I used was a map of Miami (that is the city we were in). I would mark the map using a brush dipped in India ink and ask my sales representatives where they lived and what section of Miami they worked in. If they lived in South Miami and were traveling an hour northeast to Miami Beach, they were using an hour that otherwise could have been productive time. I said, "Why don't you pretend you are limited or restricted and can sell only within a fifteen-minute drive from your home or office?" I would ask others where they lived. Then for each person I would pull out a Miami map and with India ink black out all the city except a fifteen-minute drive around their home. This was a visual, powerful reminder of the principle of focus. I would tell them, "Carry this in your car with you and concentrate on it. This is where you should prospect. This is where you choose to sell. This is where you build a network. This is where you earn your living." I also told them to study the traffic patterns in their city and make sure they were never on the streets during the busiest traffic times because that was a waste of their most valuable resource—time. I emphasized, "Focus all your time and effort in one area."

Over the years, I have been intrigued with what the Apostle Paul wrote in a letter to some first-century Christians: "This one thing I do—forgetting what is behind and straining toward what is ahead, I press on toward the goal to win the prize.... " I carry it with me on an affirmation card. It is deeply etched in my mind. *Focus! Press on!* Focus is the maximizer of success potential. It enhances creativity, increases imagination, expands vision, and multiplies inventive ability. When I am focused on successfully achieving my goals, I can dismiss worry, fear, and indecision. I have no time to dwell on the past, no time to be discouraged by what others say, think, or do. I direct all of my time and energy toward my current project.

I approach everything with full effort and attention. I know no other way. People sometimes are astonished or even amused by my intensity. I can be in a conversation or conference in my office when the phone rings, but I do not hear it. Another person walks into the room, and I do not see that individual. I am completely immersed and focused on the person and the situation before me. The ability to focus magnifies for me the urgency and excitement of the project at hand. The needed action steps emerge into camera-sharp clarity.

Think about the *opposite* of focus, the *inability* to focus on the one project you are working on at the moment:

- Can you ride two horses at once?
- Can you swim two rivers at one time?

- Can you hold two thoughts in your mind simultaneously?
- Can you participate effectively in two conversations at once?
- Can you straddle a fence indefinitely?
- Can you feel full of fear and full of faith at the same time?
- Can you get to second base with one foot planted securely on first?
- Can you fly to two different destinations at the same time?
- Can you serve two masters at one time?

Can you ride two horses at once?

The principle of focus and specialization is evident among successful people everywhere. The greatest professional athletes specialize in one sport. Doctors specialize. Lawyers specialize. A focused strategy results in sustained success and provides superior profits. For example, in the motivation companies I founded more than thirty years ago, we continue to focus and concentrate on delivering the very best products, the very best training materials, and the very best service-consciousness for helping people develop their full potential.

When I established SMI in 1960, I focused on one market—the life insurance industry—because I had a strong background and knowledge of the people and needs in that industry. Ninety percent of all the personal sales I made during the first two years after starting SMI were to the life insurance industry. I let it branch out from there. Over the years, however, over 70 percent of our sales were made with one program—*The Dynamics of Personal Motivation*. More copies of that program have been sold than the distribution of any other self-improvement program in history.

Focus! Focus! Focus!

Although photographers always give a great deal of attention to making sure their pictures are in focus, the most effective photographers also give careful attention to choosing the appropriate subject. Even if a clearly focused picture results, focusing on the wrong object produces a less than desirable picture. To provide a business analogy, you must not only "do things right" but also "do the right thing." Selecting the subject of the photo and focusing clearly on it are important to determine the quality of the finished product. To develop a habit of focus in life and to direct energy toward desired goals, learn to say "no" to certain opportunities so you can say "yes" to others.

My God-given potential has given me both the right and the responsibility to choose goals and set priorities in all areas of my life. No one else knows which goals are most appropriate for me, and no one else should dictate my priorities. Just as my father showed me how to control the awesome power of a magnifying glass and just as scientists direct the miraculous laser beam to perform incredible feats, I alone am personally responsible for my life and what I do with it. Like a laser or a sunbeam through a magnifying glass, I can burn with focused, amplified levels of energy. When I empower myself to focus on what means most to me, my success surprises even me!

10

MY EARLY STRUGGLE WITH ANGER

AS AN AUTHOR of business programs marketed in more than sixty countries, I have encountered numerous people in every culture who have shortened their careers, ambushed their futures, and stifled their personal progress because they could not handle their pent-up anger appropriately.

Our first show of anger, hostility, or defiance probably occurs as children when we do not get our way. As we become more mature, we learn to control ourselves and also to get along with people—to accept people and to be accepted by people. I personally had some difficulties. I think many of my difficulties stemmed from the fact that, emotionally, I am an intense person.

Intensity helped me to stay focused like a laser on the object of my dreams, desires, goals, and ambitions. Consequently, I resented anyone or anything that interfered with my focus.

Anger is often described as "losing one's temper" or having a "hot temper" or a "short fuse." Anger in my teens showed itself outwardly as a short fuse. I exhibited it both physically and verbally and always with great intensity. My high school coach, Coach Hill, once told me that if I did not control the intensity of my hostility and anger, I would end up in the penitentiary. But if I controlled the intensity, he said, the world would be my cornucopia. Coach Hill added that he doubted I would find it possible to live on middle ground.

I recall two of several incidents I am not proud of. Late in my elementary school years, the teacher was out of the room when a boy called me a bad name. When I in turn called him a bad name, he took out a knife and threw it at me—and missed. I picked up the knife, moved closer to him, and threw it at his foot. I did not mean to actually hurt him, but much to my surprise the knife went through his foot and into the wooden floor. I was as shocked as he was! My anger vanished immediately, and I was filled with shame and disappointment in myself. I had to pay a penalty; so I was expelled from school for a period of time and had to go to the boy's home and apologize to him and his parents. This was a painful, much-needed lesson in controlling my temper.

I never wanted to do away with my intensity because I felt it was a gift from my Creator that helped put fuel in my engine, giving me exceptional drive and energy.

On another occasion, when I was about sixteen or seventeen years old, I was visiting my girlfriend in her home. Some boys drove their car across her lawn and tore it up. Another boy and I lured them out into the country where we pulled them out of their car and shot up their car with shotguns. At no time did we intend to hurt anyone. Because of our anger and hostility, we simply wanted to get even for the damage they had done. Again, we were wrong. But sometimes an outburst of anger causes us not to think straight, and we do a second wrong. The next morning at school I was involved in a fight with one of the boys and injured him so badly that he was put in the hospital. I have never felt more remorse and disgrace about anything in my life, and I have not physically harmed another person in the last fifty years. I still feel extremely disappointed in myself and ashamed even as I share this story.

These are just two of a half dozen major incidences of mismanaged or misdirected anger in my life. I share this very personal and sensitive information in the hope that it will influence others to learn actions they can take to avoid such a notorious chapter in their own lives. Here is a simple but powerful three-step technique I used successfully in my early struggles with anger:

1. **Determine what triggers anger.** Anger begins with a *thought*—a belief that you are being unjustifiably wronged in some way. The most constructive way of controlling anger is to deal with it at this *thought level.* I force myself to identify specifically what triggers my anger. Frustration? Interruptions? Threats to my income? Someone questioning my authority or challenging my decisions? Uncooperative co-workers? Family disagreements? Whenever I feel a surge—or even a hint—of anger, I ask myself, "Why am I starting to get angry?" Once I assess or identify precisely why I feel

angry, then I can go on to the second step of handling anger.

2. **Consciously choose a constructive response to anger.** Anger causes the blood pressure to soar, the heart rate to accelerate, muscles to tense up, and the brain to go into a hostile mode or even a warlike attack mode. Before I allow myself to take any action, I consider responses that will help me to *accomplish* my goals rather than *destroy* any possibility of reaching them. To help choose the most constructive approach—the one I will be the most satisfied with in the long run—I ask myself specifically, "What results do I want to create or cause by my actions?"

   One destructive behavior I followed in the past was keeping track—making mental or even written notes—of grievances and injustices done against me. Instead, I now concentrate on *consciously choosing a constructive response.* Long ago I committed myself to read and study everything I could find on forgiveness. I learned more than simply to forgive. I learned to help people and to encourage them.

3. **Concentrate on the positive results and benefits to be gained by channeling anger constructively.** As I consider all the constructive ways I might channel my anger, I evaluate the benefits to be gained from each action. Then I select the best one and take immediate, decisive action. Focusing on the positive results and anticipating the desirable benefits of this approach fuel my motivation to take constructive actions rather than explosive, destructive ones like lashing out, blaming, or hurting others.

   Some people I know try desperately to hide, deny, suppress, or in other ways mask their angry feelings. The benefits of this approach are short-lived because it is counterproductive and self-destructive. Keeping all the pent-up anger *inside* oneself is not much better than allowing the energy to explode like misguided missiles *outside* the body. Suppressed anger creates health problems and inappropriate behavior apparently unrelated to the anger that actually causes it. Channeling anger constructively with the positive results in mind always pays off! That is why I commit myself daily to transforming any anger into actions that catapult me closer to my goals, not drive me farther away.

11

WHAT I WAS DOING WHEN . . .

MEMORIES ... my life is full of them. But I spend most of my time looking to the future, rarely to the past. When asked to share some milestone memories in my life that have shaped my attitudes and influenced who I am today, the past started reaching out and tapping me on the shoulder at every turn as I reminisced about "What I Was Doing When ..."

In 1936, when the Western Union messenger delivered the telegram that said my grandmother had died, I was eight years old. I was in the garden slicing a tomato to eat, and my mother was nearby, bringing in clothes from the outdoor clothesline. I remember vividly my mother beginning to cry as she read the telegram. She gathered me in her arms, reread the message, and continued to cry softly. Then we went indoors where Mother spent several hours telling my brother, sister, and me stories about her mother. She described how Grandmother was the matriarch in the area where she lived, serving as counselor, midwife, and helper to anyone in need.

The impact of death became a reality for me for the first time when my grandmother died. But the ancient ancestral whispers seemed to echo an even stronger reality, an eternal truth—that is, how the continuity of generations is perpetuated by our love for others and our service to them. In spite of my young age, I remember the rush of gratitude I felt for the legacy my grandmother had left.

On December 7, 1941, when Pearl Harbor was bombed, I was digging a ten-foot-by-ten-foot pit. I knew I had just about reached the ten-foot depth because my ladder was ten feet in length, and the top of it was almost even with the ground. I remember vividly being concerned that the walls of the excavation might crumble and fall in on me. Luckily, there was a great deal of caliche holding the damp, rock-pitted sides in place.

My concern about the walls collapsing was suddenly interrupted by the man who hired me; he came running over with an extension cord and a radio. He recognized the importance of the announcement being made, and he wanted me to be able to hear the historic news that Pearl Harbor had been bombed.

On May 21, 1949, when I turned twenty-one years old, I was selling insurance for Independent Life & Accident, the world's largest, most exclusive weekly premium insurance company. Eighteen months earlier I had been told I was not "cut out" for selling. But my determination, persistence, and hard work paid off. I was the number one producer by the time I turned twenty-one. This milestone memory is just one of many that reminds me of the fact that self-motivation is the power that raises people to any level they seek.

On March 13, 1950, when my first son, Jim, was born, I was selling life insurance at the hospital to other people waiting for the arrival of their babies. A gentleman named Mr. Beach bought a policy, and I made a $650 commission on the premium. My compelling desire was to impart to him and other parents the responsibility of making sure that the futures of their newborn babies were financially secure—and to earn enough commission to cover expenses for my own son's birth.

The miracle of birth, especially of my first son, touched me with a kind of timelessness—a sense that life fulfills and extends itself through these tiny bundles of humanity. "This is how life begins," I thought to myself that memorable day, "small and dependent upon parents to help make the most of this new life." I feel fairly good about having upheld my end of the deal as a parent, and I feel even more certain that Jim has upheld his. As an outstanding attorney with a well-earned reputation for excellence, Jim has always assumed responsibility for his life and made the most of his potential.

In 1956, when I was 27, I made my first million dollars selling life insurance and had figured out how to do everything faster than average. I noticed that I was on a faster career track than most people in my age group:

- At age twenty-one, I led the largest weekly premium insurance company.
- At twenty-two, I qualified as the youngest member of the Million Dollar Round Table.
- At twenty-four, I was making more money than any other salesperson in the insurance business.
- At twenty-six, I built one of the largest life insurance agencies in America.
- At twenty-seven, I had made my first million dollars.

Embarrassed is how I feel when admitting that making the first million was so easy for me. I remember thinking, "So what? Where do I go from here?" I simply did not have a passion for that business even though I could do it exceedingly well. For the first time in my life, it struck me that just because someone can perform a job well is not a valid reason for staying in that career. True indicators that a person has chosen the right career are a burning fervor, a driving desire, a sense of mission, and a purpose. I am glad I switched careers; my second million dollars—and subsequent millions—were earned more slowly but with a compelling and satisfying sense of mission and purpose.

In 1953, I coined the often quoted statement that begins "Whatever you vividly imagine..." I was at the School of Business at Purdue University attending a class on wills, trusts, and estate planning. This was, of course, before I started SMI. The professor asked me to give a talk about my success in the insurance business and how I had done so much although I was so young. In that speech I first used these words, which encapsulate my philosophy for success: "Whatever you vividly imagine, ardently desire, sincerely believe, and enthusiastically act upon must inevitably come to pass!"

On November 22, 1963, when John F. Kennedy was assassinated, I was in the conference center of a hotel in Waco, Texas, with twenty Japanese business executives.

I remember it vividly. The night before, just at dusk, I went out to the Waco Airport to meet a DC-3 airplane and greet twenty Japanese business executives who had come all the way from Tokyo to receive training on the new leadership course that we had just produced in Japanese. They also came to look over our company and plant and make arrangements for additional expansion of our product line and distribution systems. What I remember most about greeting them was seeing the joy and excitement on their faces as we handed each of them a Texas cowboy hat!

When we received the news about President Kennedy, the Japanese were shocked, stunned, and rendered speechless, as were those of us conducting the seminar. We stopped the meeting. We took the rest of the afternoon off and met for dinner at Ridgewood Country Club. It was a sad evening in one way because of our fallen leader—the American president who provided strong, decisive leadership in the midst of a worldwide cold war. The youngest of any of our United States presidents,

Twenty Japanese business executives enjoy their cowboy hats I gave to them when they arrived in Waco, Texas, to receive training on the PJM leadership program that had just been produced in Japanese.

he set lofty goals, such as putting a man on the moon, and then inspired people to meet those incredible goals.

In other ways, it was an insightful, comforting evening, because the hard-hitting Japanese businesspeople displayed so much concern and compassion. As we sat in a room together, we were reminded that we are all members of a global village and that our countries' destinies are inextricably intertwined.

On December 6, 1963, when I received a telephone call that my father had died, I was in Dr. Walter Hunter's dental chair. The thought flashed through my mind that the last time I had seen my father was October 19, 1962, and the last words I spoke to him were lines from a poem. I'm not sure the name of this poem or its author, but it is one that both of us had discussed and loved:

We face the sunrise…
We turn our backs and forget the past.
Our tomorrow will not be trampled
by the heavy hooves of yesterday.

We defy precedent . . .
We prove the impossible.
We're motivators with a mission . . .
We are God's answer to the commonplace.
Unbroken, untamed and unafraid,
We challenge custom, we welcome change.

We abhor the beaten path.
Not for us the cowbell or the curfew.
We shun the smooth highroad
Strung with signs of warning and safety signals.
We dare the dark to reach the dawn.

We abandon the chilly caverns of caution.
If we are missing, you will find our bones out yonder in the sun with our arms outstretched toward the great Tomorrow.

When the 1964 Olympics were held in Tokyo in 1964, I had just completed a trip to Japan and Asia. While in Japan I worked to help get our business going in that country. I had also done some personal selling and recruiting in Hong Kong. The Olympics were organized to encourage world peace and friendship and to promote amateur athletics. Our business reminds me of the Olympics: We, too, are dedicated to "motivating people to their full potential."® I remember thinking that summer in Japan how I intended to do all I could to promote the spirit of the Olympics in all areas of my life and in the lives of others—truly a Total Person Olympics.

On July 6, 1969, when my mother died, I was holding her hand. She had served faithfully and lovingly as my friend, my confidante, my encourager, and my researcher—a role model par excellence. Two weeks before my mother died at eighty years young, she was still helping others. She was raising money for the *City of Hope*—a large ship outfitted as a hospital and traveling to ports of countries where basic medical treatment was a luxury. Its livelihood depended on the generosity of others.

When asked why she was still working to raise money for *City of Hope*, she responded, "If I don't do it, who will?" This response was characteristic of her heartfelt sense of responsibility to help others in whatever way she could—large or small. I still have the piece of paper I found in her apron pocket on which she had written, "City of Hope—seven cents."

On January 28, 1986, a few brief moments after takeoff, the space shuttle "*Challenger*" was destroyed, with no survivors. Christa McAuliffe, the first teacher to be chosen for a space flight, was among the fatalities. Her spirit of adventure and commitment to learning had endeared her to people around the world, especially to our daughter Leslie then ten years old. At the time of takeoff, Leslie was enjoying a session with her tutor while we were spending the winter months in the Cayman Islands. Jane and I were at the office working. Leslie called us to tell us about the disaster and pleaded for us to come home to watch the newscast of this awful tragedy with her. We three and her tutor watched and cried with the rest of the world as the newscast informed us of what had happened.

Shocked, our thoughts first focused on the unthinkable, the reality of this catastrophe. And then we struggled to make sense of it all. Emerging in our thoughts was the relative insignificance of things, the inestimable value of people, and the power of the undauntable human spirit to survive any disaster—and to emerge even stronger simply because we have overcome.

In November 1989, when the Berlin Wall was opened, I was totally immersed in all of the demands of the forty-plus businesses I had begun. I have a little chunk of concrete from the Berlin Wall mounted in a shadow box on a wall in my home. It is a reminder to me of the freedom I enjoy to pursue various business interests. It also reminds me that the most prohibitive and destructive walls are those in our minds; nothing is worse than an imprisoned mind and spirit. The greatest freedom comes from tearing walls down and refusing to let any barriers keep me from being what my Creator intended me to be.

As I reminisce about my life, I am struck anew with the realization that what has happened to me in the past is not nearly as important as what I do with my life in the future. Reflecting on my life and what I was doing when some of life's momentous events occurred provides the assurance that my future can be what I make of it. The choice is mine. A familiar proverb reminds me that now is the time to get started: "Today is the first day of the rest of your life."

12

HAPPEN-CHANCE MEETINGS

"No man is an island, entire of itself."

THESE WELL-KNOWN WORDS penned by English poet John Donne were never truer than when applied to my life. Over the decades, I have met numerous illustrious people. Many of these happen-chance meetings have influenced decisions *I* have made as well as decisions *they* have made. By "happen-chance," I mean unplanned *chance* meetings, *coincidental* meetings, *accidental* meetings, *serendipitous* meetings, *fortuitous* meetings. Most of us have experienced these kinds of encounters—the kind where we were instrumental in creating a change in *someone else's life*, or they created change in *our lives*. I would like to share some of my most memorable happen-chance meetings and the unique circumstances surrounding them.

One of our distributors and I were at lunch one day when I asked him some questions, such as whom had he worked for before coming with us. In the question and answer process, he said it was strange—no one else had directed this particular set of questions to him before. He added, "You have really started me thinking. Could I talk to you again tomorrow?"

At our meeting the next day he said, "You know, I have met no one I respect more. I love these programs your company produces. But I am just now discovering my real reason for joining you was that I had no guts! There is a lot I want to do, but I was afraid because I've always worked for a big company. Now, since I have this Plan of Action, I am getting the courage and backbone to stand up and speak up." Numerous in-depth conversations with him, and some soul-searching on his own, resulted in his setting a goal to leave our company to start his own computer company... and he did just that!

This former distributor of ours called me about five years later. He shared with me the success his business had enjoyed before he finally sold it for several million dollars and retired. He said, "I don't know what I would have done, and it scares me to think what would have happened to me if I hadn't asked you to have lunch with me that day at the hotel." He added, "That happen-chance meeting changed the direction of my life."

A man who pulled my car out of a ditch I had plunged into during a blinding downpour provides another memorable happen-chance meeting. I was driving from Valdosta to Tifton, Georgia, when a sudden deluge caused me to spin off the road into a ditch. I climbed out and up an embankment to an old, unpainted farmhouse about fifty feet away. A man met me at the door, and I explained my dilemma to him. The gracious man cranked up his tractor and pulled my car out of the ditch. Because the rain was still extremely heavy, I gladly accepted an invitation to "stay in until the weather improves." We enjoyed a congenial conversation, and before the rain stopped, I had recruited him into the insurance business.

My newfound friend became highly successful in his new career. In his first year he sold over two million dollars (face value) in permanent life insurance—an almost unprecedented feat at that time. I recall the sense of excitement and deep satisfaction I felt in seeing the success that this man achieved. He pulled my *car* out of a ditch, but he later told me, "You pulled my *life* out of a ditch."

A hitchhiker I met in another happen-chance meeting quickly transformed himself into a contest winner. My good friend Bill Armor was driving along a Florida highway when he picked up a hitchhiker from New Jersey; his name was Larry Leavitt. Slovenly dressed and unshaven, Leavitt had just suffered through a divorce. Bill brought him to me because my philosophy was well known, "We don't judge people; we give them an opportunity to prove themselves."

Bill Armor and I helped Leavitt "clean up his life" and took him to Bill's insurance agency where a seventy-seven-day sales contest was in progress. Leavitt won first place in the contest! My philosophy of believing in people and encouraging them to do their best paid off again. I can still hear Larry Leavitt declaring, "*Someone had faith in me!*"

Another providential happen-chance meeting was the wife of a prospect I had called on. When I called on the Duggans at their home in Miami, Florida, I learned that Mr. Duggan had been injured in an automobile accident. It did not take long talking to Mrs. Duggan for me to conclude that she had the potential to become a top salesperson. So I recruited her to sell insurance. She not only fulfilled my expectations, she surpassed them. She proved highly productive, attaining membership in the Million Dollar Round Table. She continued to win recognition as a top producer in the company. Mrs. Duggan invested her earnings in prebuilt condominiums on the Florida coast and became a millionaire. I have often wondered what would have happened to her life had I not called on her husband to sell *him* insurance but instead recruited *her* to sell insurance.

An iron lung was the focal point of another happen-chance meeting. John Cook had polio, and the doctors had told him he would be in that iron lung for the rest of his life. The state of John's life was dismal at the time I met him.

I had hired John's wife, Sarah, as my part-time secretary. One day she came to work crying, telling me she had just had an automobile accident, had a one-year-old toddler at home, and her husband had polio and was in an iron lung. I went to meet John and to visit with him. Even though Sarah had told me he was in an iron lung, I was astonished when I saw him for the first

This picture taken in 1960 shows John Cook (center), my first employee. Sarah, John's wife, is beside him, and I am at the far right.

time. During our conversation he told me what the doctor had said—that he would be in the iron lung the rest of his life.

Being the positive person that I am—and the optimist—I immediately started encouraging John. I remember telling him, "I think that decision is not up to the doctors. It depends on your personal faith and the faith and prayers of Sarah. Your recovery depends on your determination and on what you do with your life." Only a short while after that, John was out of the iron lung, wearing braces. John's turnaround recovery can be attributed to the tremendous support of Sarah, John's own internal fortitude, and the faith both had in God that John would recover. The story of John's miraculous recovery later appeared in *Guidepost* magazine. Although John's recovery required a couple of years, it seemed like an absolute miracle to everybody who saw this transformation.

My admiration and respect for John Cook was so great that when I started SMI I wanted John to help me run it. So John became my first employee. That was one of the happiest happen-chance meetings I have ever experienced, because it provided me an excellent employee for years and a lifelong friend in John Cook.

A fellow working on a Coca-Cola truck provided another happen-chance meeting with long-lasting consequences. The day I met Rex Hodges was October 6, 1952. I remember the date because the World Series was going on. I was in a small store where Rex was making a Coca-Cola delivery. The radio was blaring out the World Series, and I noticed Rex was paying close attention to the game. I invited Rex to take a break and watch some of the game with me on my television set at home. He accepted my offer, and we finished watching the exciting game at my house.

The more I talked to Rex, the more I recognized his extensive unused potential. He was mentally sharp, and he had a genuine interest in people. Rex Hodges, like me, had been in the military service, and we were about the same age. I explained to Rex what I did and how gratifying it was for me to be able to help people. I told him he could take advantage of the same opportunity, and it could change his life forever. And that's how I recruited him into my insurance agency.

Rex Hodges's life was, indeed, changed forever—he has been extremely successful in the insurance industry. He became a member of the Million Dollar Round Table and has enjoyed a satisfying career with Franklin Life for over forty years. He has also been a pillar in the community, including his church, and he has been an exemplary family man, having reared several fine children. Just another happen-chance meeting!

A man born with a silver spoon in his mouth provided another remarkable happen-chance meeting. When I picked up hitch-hiker Al Watson, he was wearing a sweater with "PC" on it. The "PC" stood for Presbyterian College in South Carolina, where he was a student. Al told me about his life—that he was born with a silver spoon in his mouth and that he had never learned what work was. He lamented the fact that he did not know how to do anything and said he wished he had been born with nothing so he would have been forced to learn how to work.

Because Al seemed so distressed that he did not know how to work, I decided to show him how to fish or cut bait. So one day I asked him to please give me his wallet, or at least all the money in his wallet. At the same time I wanted him to see that I was taking all of the money out of my wallet, except five dollars. I said that we were going to leave the money at the house, we were going to get in the car, and we were going to drive until we were out of gas. Then we were going to have to sell something to get gas, to get a place to sleep, and to get some food. I told him, "You're going to learn how to do what you have to do when you have to do it." We got as far as Tifton, Georgia, a town so backward that it still had "selling blocks" (for slaves) in the center of the town square. Our five dollars was gone. When the money ran out, it was *performance time*. We did not just *need* to sell an insurance policy, we were *going* to sell an insurance policy—no ifs, ands, or buts! If we had to knock on every door in the town until the middle of the night to get someone to listen and to get a prospect, that was what was going to happen.

Al started on one side of the street and I started on the other side, going business to business. I did not do so well! I visited five or six stores with no results. I was sitting on the curb, when all of a sudden Al came out of a building waving nine dollars. He was the most excited young man I had ever seen in my life. He had sold a one thousand dollar life insurance policy with a quarterly premium of nine dollars. Al was euphoric! I said, "How did it go?" He replied, "Selling the policy was easy. Having him give me nine dollars cash instead of a check was difficult!"

The next day we got up like we owned the world. We knew we were going to have a great day and a great week! We sold over ten policies that week, got cash for most of them, and went back to Columbus, Georgia, with a briefcase full of applications. Both of us stood a little taller, with more confidence and more experience.

Within a few years Al became a member of the Million Dollar Round Table. When he accomplished this milestone, he wrote to me even before writing to his family, because, as he put it, I was his "mentor, teacher, and motivator." Al Watson told me that he was thankful that he had met me and commented, "You really showed me just how much influence one person can have on the life of someone else."

A volatile church committee meeting on finance was the setting for a fortunate happen-chance meeting. The discussion in the church committee meeting seemed to be going nowhere until one man stood up to speak. He was calm, soft spoken, and his thoughts were clearly organized. I concluded right then, "Here's a man I would like to be in business with."

Because my "seize the day" attitude had served me well in previous situations, I put it to use; immediately at the conclusion of the meeting I introduced myself to this highly effective individual. Soon after that I offered him an opportunity with my companies, and now more than thirty years later, he is still associated with them. His name is Joe Baxter, and he is the president of International Achievement, the company that owns Success Motivation International, Leadership Motivation International, and Family Motivation International. He and his wife, Bessie, have traveled all over the world to seventy-five countries, setting up international leaders for our marketing companies.

A church pew was the site of a happen-chance meeting that resulted in recruiting another executive for my companies. The first steps of the recruitment process of Dr. Barbara Chesser, president of our product development company, Success Motivation, Inc., began when I asked Jane about a couple who sat on the same pew with us at church. When Jane told me their names, I remembered reading an article that week in *Reader's Digest* by Dr. Chesser. I soon found out that she had a prestigious position at Baylor University. Just as in Joe Baxter's case, people would say, "Forget her—she wouldn't want to change positions." She appeared to be unassertive and unassuming and was small in stature—not exactly a stereotypical executive.

But I have never been one to assume anything nor to be swayed by what others say, think, or do. So I invited Barbara and her husband, Del, to go to lunch with us. I told Barbara we were looking for someone with editorial skills to join us in our product development company. I discovered quickly she not only had incredible editorial skills, but she had also traveled and worked internationally. She had extensive management skills in her twenty-plus years with university teaching and administration; she had stamina, a strong work ethic, and a philosophy unbelievably supportive of my dedication to "motivating people to their full potential."® Barbara has just recently celebrated her tenth anniversary with my companies.

I have given several examples of "happen-chance" meetings. I know there is the possibility that a reader who depends solely on the dictionary would say that the title should have been "happenstance meetings." But that is what I like about writing…I can make my own words and craft them to say what I want to say.

13

"HOW DO YOU GET AHEAD AROUND HERE?"

THIS QUESTION WAS ASKED of me by Ferrell Hunter in 1961. At that time he had just married and moved to Central Texas to work for Success Motivation Institute, Inc., the first company of the Meyer Family Enterprises. Ferrell started work packing boxes in the warehouse for $2.65 an hour.

One day we were having a conversation, and he asked, "How do you get ahead around here?" I remember very clearly what I told him.

Number One: Do More Than You Get Paid For

I was reared to do the best I could, to believe that the primary consideration was not what I was paid. I believed my most important considerations were productivity, efficiency, and effectiveness. Early in my life I developed the keen sense of responsibility and obligation to be fruitful and profitable for my employer every hour, every day. This philosophy has served me well, and as I have observed others who got ahead in their careers, I have seen this philosophy hold true. For the last forty years, I think the best advice I have ever given young people is to always do more than you get paid for.

In contrast to doing more than you get paid for, today a culture springing from the 1950s and 1960s seems to be common. A comedian I saw at a dinner theater demonstrated this culture. The setting was a restaurant looking for some new employees. A disheveled young man responded to the advertisement; when he came in to talk to the manager, he said, "Hey, you the boss? Come here." The owner responded, "Yes, are you looking for a job?" The young man said, "I don't know. I need to ask you some questions first. How much time do we get off during the day for breaks? How much vacation time do we get? How much sick leave do we get, and what are the other benefits?"

"Well, come in," the owner said, "and let's talk about the job." The young applicant said, "I don't want to know about the job until you answer my questions."

The skit was exaggerated, but it made an indelible impression on me—a frightening one at that because I see it lived out over and over and over by young people, male and female, for all kinds of jobs.

Teachers who are friends of mine tell me there is a similar attitude from students in the classroom. When an assignment is made, students often ask questions like, "How wide can the margins be? What's the minimum number of pages? Can we use double spacing instead of single spacing?" and "Can we triple space in between paragraphs?" There seems to be an emphasis on setting the teacher up so that a minimum of everything is acceptable—a minimum of thinking, a minimum of working, a minimum of writing—an all-out effort to get by with the least possible amount of exertion, output, or productivity.

Make no mistake, employees and prospective employees need to make sure they know what is expected of them—the job description, objectives, duties, responsibilities. Only when they know what is expected can they meet those expectations—and then some. I can remember telling Ferrell that doing more than you get paid for always pays off. Some practical applications of this attitude include these:

- Take pride in your work.
- Always make sure it is "better than average."
- Get to work early, not "just in time"—and *never* late.
- Stay after hours if necessary to get the job done well and on time.
- Identify existing problems and seek solutions—either solve the problem or offer suggested remedies to the appropriate person.
- Assume responsibility for your work, including your mistakes. Never place blame on others for problems.

Ferrell took my advice and put it into action from the very beginning. From his example, I have drawn other suggestions that support my "do more than you get paid for" philosophy. For example, make yourself visible from the beginning. First impressions are always important, and a fast start on a new job can program your whole career for success—not just when you are starting out but any time you change jobs. The faster you rise, the higher you aim. Conversely, a plodding start induces lower expectations. First impressions are also important because the judgments of your supervisors, whether accurate or not, become self-fulfilling prophecies. Doing more than you get paid for requires a fast start and keeping up that pace with the determination to do your best and reach your goals.

Number Two: Overfill Your Place

Start looking around, I emphasized to Ferrell, and find out what jobs are done within visual distance of where you are working.

- How does the shipping department operate?
- How are all the mailing lists handled?
- Who do the people in the other departments report to and why?
- How does all the equipment around here work?

"Trust me," I emphasized to Ferrell, "if you do more than you get paid for and you start overfilling your place, management will notice that you know everybody else's job in your department. There soon will be a change in your pay, and you will be promoted. It is inevitable." I told Ferrell that you are never promoted when no one else knows your current job. The best basis for advancement is to organize yourself out of every job you are put into. You simply cannot take this advice and not get ahead around here.

I gave this same advice to our eldest daughter, Janna, when she started working at one of our companies. She began as a secretarial assistant, and then job-by-job, function-by-function, she learned them and mastered them and was promoted to executive assistant to the president of the company. Janna became an indispensable person because she knew everybody else's job, she knew all the files, she knew where everything was. When anyone wanted to know anything, they always asked Janna. *Overfilling your place* always pays off.

Number Three: Learn What the Company Does

I remember Ferrell asking about other opportunities. In addition, he became a student of administration, supervision, and management. He took all of the courses we had and read everything else he could get his hands on—books and newsletters. He attended seminars, conclaves, and conventions.

Ferrell never stopped learning everything he could about our company, but he also learned what the competition was doing and then offered ideas for improving our products, service, inventory control and shipping, etc.

I have always maintained that asking questions is a great way to learn. Evidently Ferrell felt the same way because he asked lots of questions of everybody. He got to know everybody in every department, in every area of the operation. He would ask them, "Exactly what do you do in this job?" Ferrell soon became a quick and authoritative information source. The simplicity of question asking was amazing—to me and to Ferrell. As Ferrell put it, "It isn't even hard, but the results are phenomenal."

When Ferrell first started working for our company, we had twelve-inch, long-playing records with the printed scripts. This was in the days before cassette tapes and portable recorders. Even though Ferrell's job was to assemble the programs we produced, he began taking some of the programs home with him and listening to the records after hours. Before long he had gone through a dozen of them. He knew the material well. I could see the evidence in his life. He was becoming a "product of the product." He knew the material so well that in addition to using it in his own personal life and applying the principles within the company, he offered to teach them. When I asked him, "Would you like to do one of the training sessions at our school?" he jumped at the opportunity! At the same time, his income jumped.

On another occasion I told Ferrell I was getting ready to conduct some innovative leadership workshops to approximately one hundred audiences around the United States and overseas. I asked Ferrell if he would like to accompany me and do part of the sessions. He felt he was qualified and ready to assume that responsibility. We did (and he did) an exemplary job. We received some of the highest ratings on our evaluation sheets we had ever received since starting the company. Ferrell scored as high or higher than anyone else in the company. His learning what our company does had catapulted him quickly to a high level of satisfying success. There is a saying I have heard for years that applies to my suggestion to learn what the company does: "When you are through learning, you are through."

Number Four: Ask for More to Do

Ferrell quickly gained greater self-confidence, enhanced self-image, improved managerial skills, and increased communication skills—both written and speaking. One day he surprised me when he asked, "What else can I do?" I was amazed at his question but also very thankful. We started giving Ferrell more than one job to do. He was involved in management, training schools, public speaking, and making some significant contributions to product development. What happened as a result of his asking for more to do? His span of involvement in our companies broadened, and his income went up.

A fellow employee, obviously a little jealous of Ferrell's advancement, said to Ferrell, "You're just lucky." Ferrell was always thinking on his feet, and this time was no exception. He quickly replied, "I am a great believer in luck. The harder I work, the more of it I seem to have."

Number Five: Ask for More Responsibility

Ferrell never stopped asking for more to do. At one time he was involved in helping to manage as many as twelve Meyer family companies. When Ferrell demonstrated capability and credibility in his current responsibility, he would ask for more responsibility in line with his interests and abilities and in line with what he thought would improve our products and service.

Ferrell Hunter began early in his career with a positive attitude toward using more of his potential. Learning to speak to groups was one of his most difficult challenges. Accepting that challenge, he maintains now, has been well worth his efforts. Ferrell is seen here making a presentation to the national board of a well-known civic organization.

The amazing capacity to shift gears was one of Ferrell's strengths. He developed that strength as he carried out my other suggestions for getting ahead. He could go from one meeting to the next and from one building to the next and be totally attentive, contributing worthwhile information to each company. Ferrell's insights and suggestions were always helpful. His usual first question always drove straight to the heart of a matter: "What's the goal here?"

Number Six: Cross Train

It has always astounded me that companies will select good people, give them responsibility and authority in a specific position in a company, and then almost "pigeonhole" them where they remain in that function and are never given an opportunity to learn other job functions and responsibilities in the company. What has made our group of companies strong is the enormous amount of cross training we have done over the last thirty years. All of our top people could be put in almost any position in any company and operate and run it professionally.

Ferrell has been one of my most diligent students of cross training. On average, we have changed his title and position every twenty-four months for the past thirty years. He has packed boxes. He has supervised others who have packed boxes. He has been a manager of a department and of several companies. He has been vice president of training. He has been president of marketing companies, manufacturing companies, and a long list of other companies.

In the past few years we have used Ferrell in the capacity of a consultant for a trustee group that helps manage more than forty Meyer Enterprises companies. Ferrell is currently working as a CEO for a group of over half a dozen companies owned by my brother and me. These companies are mainly in the automotive parts manufacturing business—some in the U.S. and some in foreign countries. Because of the cross training Ferrell received over the past thirty years, making the transition to head up a totally different type of business was easy for him.

I have told Ferrell's story over and over to young people as an encouragement and to tell them, "Life may be hard by the yard, but it's a cinch by the inch." Ferrell's example demonstrates that success is a *journey*—you do it by climbing one step at a time and one day at a time. It is not done overnight. When it is done right and with depth, as Ferrell has done it, anyone can do the same thing, starting at any company, anywhere, any time, in any position.

In our companies over a thirty-five-year period, there are very few positions with which Ferrell has not helped. He worked with our international business and traveled all over the world—on every continent—and in almost every major city—helping and assisting. I have often wondered if Ferrell has ever considered how powerful and how pivotal that question has been for him and how it can open doors of opportunity for anyone, anywhere, who follows the guidelines outlined to answer the question: "How do you get ahead around here?"

14

NOTEPADS EVERYWHERE

"Write it Down! Write it Down! Write it Down!"

ON THE BEACH outside the Pierre Marquez and Princess Hotel in Acapulco, Mexico, you can walk south for miles and see few buildings and rarely run into another person. I was taking a walk on this beautiful beach when I saw someone in the distance walking toward me. Knowing I would make an attempt to meet him and get his name, address, and phone number, I was alarmed. I was wearing only a bathing suit, so how could I record this information? I began frantically to look for something to write on—and found a piece of cardboard and a little chunk of lipstick. Armed with this substitute notepad and pen, I was prepared to meet him. I continued walking in his direction, met him, and enjoyed a friendly chat. As I had anticipated, he told me his name and address. With my makeshift writing gear, I wrote down this information about my newfound friend. We corresponded for several months. Then he became associated with one of our marketing companies and eventually became a leading distributor for more than ten years.

It is easy to understand why I have an obsession *always* to be prepared to write down information. Thinking about where my life would be now if I had not acquired this success habit scares me! Countless experiences have convinced me that everyone is creative and all people have an incredible capacity for imagination, innovation, and productivity if they simply develop the habit of using it. Writing down information is one of the most effective ways to develop one's full creative capacity. Writing crystallizes thought, and crystallized thought motivates effective, focused action. When I put my ideas in writing, I refine them, I think of ways I can put them to good use, and my motivation grows and compels me to purposeful action! When, for instance, I jot down someone's name and address, I can contact them later if I want to—just as I contacted the gentleman I met on that beach in Acapulco.

Watching my mother inspired me to develop the habit of always having something to write on and something to write with. I never once saw her when she did not have access to paper and pencil—no matter where or what the occasion. Capturing an idea, recording a thought, or outlining a plan on a notecard is now a habit with me. I keep three-by-five cards in my bathroom. I store three-by-five cards in the drawer of our nightstand. I place three-by-five cards and a notepad by our television set. I carry three-by-five cards in my pocket wherever I go. I take cards, tablets, or notepads whenever and wherever I travel. As Jane exuberantly expressed it once, "Paul has *notepads everywhere*!"

On another occasion I was riding my bicycle when I stopped under a shade tree to have a drink of water. A faded and slightly rusted real estate sign with a phone number on it was lying on the ground. I looked at the property, compared it to the properties on both sides of it, and thought, "Everything is built up around here except this one piece of property. Why so?"

With my ever-present pencil and paper, I wrote down the telephone number on the sign and headed for home. When I called the number I had written down, the person answering the phone said my questions were a waste of time. The property was in litigation and had been for over ten years. I insisted, "Check and see if it is still in litigation." The real estate agent called and found out the lien had been lifted just the week before. My next question was, "Do you know who owns it?" He replied, "Yes, but he lives in another state." I responded, "Please contact him and see if he wants to sell it." He replied, "I don't think he will." Growing impatient, I emphasized, "We aren't going to know unless we ask, are we?" So he called and asked—and the owner said he would sell it. Within a week I had the property under contract. The word got out in the surrounding area that the property was under contract. I had no idea what its actual value was, but I was offered a huge profit over what I had the contract for.

Everybody calls me lucky, but I do not think my success is mere luck. How many people would move the debris off an old sign, write the number down, and call it? Success requires awareness, initiative, and comprehending the power of having pen and paper handy at all times. (By the way, that property tripled its value in a four-year period.)

At least three out of seven nights a week I wake up in the middle of the night with a creative idea either for one of our SMI or LMI courses or for one of our family courses. The first draft of the number-one self-improvement course in the world over the last thirty-five years was written this way. The genesis of this far-reaching program occurred under a palm tree at two o'clock in the morning. I had been incubating and nurturing thoughts for it for some time, but writing it out occurred like a revelation to me. I could see in my mind's eye the title of the program, the lesson titles, the outline, and the contents. Victor Hugo, world-renowned author of several classic novels such as *Les Misérables*, once said something like, "There is one thing stronger than all the armies in the world, and that is an idea whose time has come."

Evidently the time had come for *The Dynamics of Personal Motivation* to be written because I wrote as fast as humanly possible for several hours. I had to scurry back to my room to get more notepads. My hand grew numb from writing information on page after page as it came off the tape reels of my mind that night. *The Dynamics of Personal Motivation* has been translated into more than a dozen languages and marketed in sixty countries for more than thirty years with only a half dozen updates and revisions. Again, having pen and *notepads everywhere* paid off!

For several years I have invested in real estate and enjoyed the sense of accomplishment that comes from successful ventures. My most satisfying real estate project is a beautiful complex I designed myself. I sketched the design for the building on a notepad I always carry with me in the car. The concept for the overall design as well as ideas for the myriad details struck me almost simultaneously. I remember thinking to myself, "Write it down! Write it down! Write it down!"

I captured the ideas as completely and rapidly as I humanly could—the floor plan, the design for the different units to provide the most privacy, and the unusual angles of the balconies and windows to take advantage of the magnificent view. When the contractor reviewed my plans, he was amazed at their ingenuity, intricacy, and accuracy.

A notepad, flashlight, and pen have been purposely placed by my bed for the last forty-five years. I awaken some nights once, some nights several times, writing down every single idea. Later,

I categorize the ideas and file them to use for future research. Sometimes I never use the ideas myself but instead give them to someone I know can use them. At other times I have actually gift wrapped certain notes and sent them to someone I know is looking for good ideas.

An article I read recently, and took notes on, reported that every person spends an average of eight years of his or her life waiting—waiting for traffic lights to change, waiting for connecting flights, waiting for the subway, waiting in the doctor's office, or waiting for other kinds of appointments.

To maximize the use of the many hours I spend flying, I always have my pencil and pad or notecards for writing out good ideas that can be generated in otherwise wasted time.

First of all, I make it a point to schedule my time to minimize waiting. But when waiting is unavoidable, I circumvent the counterproductive tension created by waiting with nothing to do. I always have my pad and pencil or notecards for writing out good ideas that can be generated in otherwise wasted time.

Nowadays I also carry a small handheld recorder. Then depending on the situation, I preserve my thoughts with pen and paper or with my portable recorder. Creative tension generated by waiting has produced some of my best ideas ever. Writing them down has helped me write my own ticket to success many times. When the good ideas come or other opportunities present themselves, I am going to be prepared with my portable recorder, with notecards, or with *notepads everywhere!*

15

THREE STRIKES—BUT NOT OUT

In baseball, three strikes make an out. Throughout the years of my life I have escaped some dangerous, hair-raising circumstances. I have been extremely fortunate to be spared from numerous life-threatening situations. Three narrow escapes in airplanes suggested to me the title for this story, "Three Strikes—But Not Out!"

Flying from Waco, Texas, to Atlanta, Georgia, in a Bonanza airplane provides one frightening example in which I almost struck out. We ran into some bad weather so we were trying to stay below the one-hundred-foot ceiling. But we were near mountains, our gas tank was almost empty, and it was getting dark fast! We were obviously lost and off course. The pilot had few hours of flying time. I remember that he, the other passenger, and I frantically explored our best options. The other passenger and I had been talking and not paying attention to the pilot's flying. But we both insisted we should stay low since we could not use instruments to guide us; at least we could follow a road.

That road led us to Starkville, Mississippi. The reason I knew it was Starkville was, by that time, the ceiling was under one hundred feet and as we went by a water tank, I could read the name of the town on the side of the tank. I was concerned that we were going to run into a tower or something else while we were looking for a place to land. The fact that it was turning dark rapidly did not help the situation. Before we could find a suitable place to land, the gas tank hit empty, the engine stopped, and we crash-landed in a field near a school. Considering the circumstances, it was actually a pretty good landing.

We were momentarily stunned, but miraculously nobody was hurt. I told the pilot I would take my suitcase and walk to the nearby road to hitchhike to the next town so I could catch a bus to Atlanta, Georgia. "No hard feelings," I told the pilot, "but I am not going to get back in an airplane with you ever again." Strike one—*but still at bat*.

On another occasion I was in Minneapolis, Minnesota, assisting a friend who owned a manufacturing company. He needed some marketing ideas, and I was giving him the benefit of some of my experience in that area. He asked me to fly to Cincinnati, Ohio. I said to him, "Lend me your airplane, and I'll go." His airplane was a single-engine Navion. It was in the shop and had been overhauled but had not been checked out. I took off for Cincinnati, landing once in Wisconsin. I ran into some bad weather near Chicago, but by two o'clock in the afternoon the weather cleared. My brother, Carl, who was accompanying me, was hungry and wanted a sandwich. I thought, "We'll just land here, grab a bite to eat, and gas up." As our plane started to touch down, we discovered there was no hydraulic system—no brakes! Because the grass field we wanted to land in was too short, we took off back into the air. But the controls no longer worked, and we crashed in a cornfield!

One wing was crushed and mangled, and considerable damage was done to other parts of the airplane. We were indeed truly lucky to escape virtually unharmed except for a gash in my elbow. We walked to an old farmhouse on the property, and an elderly man came to the door. I said to him, "I just wanted to tell you that I crashed in your field."

He responded, "My name is Shroud." (I was happy that I had no personal need for a "shroud" after that crash.) I told him my name, and he answered, "Glad to have you."

"I crashed in your field out here and plowed up some of your corn," I said to him. "I just wanted to tell you I'd pay for it."

"That's good," he said. Carl was standing behind the farmer and laughing at both of us as our conversation steadily grew funnier. It became obvious that the farmer was almost deaf. So we left and walked back to the airport and the FBO (Field Base Operation), told the young man who operated it what had happened, and asked if we could use his phone. Because my elbow was hurting, Carl used the phone to talk to my friend in Minneapolis. Carl told him we had a problem landing in Indiana. All I could hear was my brother's side of the conversation. Carl said, "No. No, I don't think we can fly it today." I also remember hearing Carl say, "No, I don't know how much it would cost to fix it. I've been in the trucking business." Next I heard Carl say, "No, I don't think we can get it fixed in time to leave tomorrow."

Now it was my turn to laugh at the conversation and the absurdity of the situation. Why, at least two or three weeks would be required to repair the plane! It would have to be picked up with a large truck, dismantled, and rebuilt. Not once did the owner of the plane—my friend—ask about our physical condition; he concentrated all his attention and concern on his airplane. That was strike two—*but still at bat*.

On another occasion, I was flying with three other men in an airplane. One of the men in the back of the plane was telling a joke. The pilot was listening intently to the joke and laughing as the fellow was nearing the punch line. Suddenly it dawned on the pilot that he had forgotten to put the landing gear down. By the time the pilot reacted, the plane had already touched down on the runway of the large Birmingham International Airport.

You have never heard such a racket in your life as that plane made sliding along the concrete pavement. Sparks were flying

I never take any chances with weather or allow any distractions to pull my attention away from flying. I always use extreme caution.

everywhere! The plane did not go very far before it came to a stop; it had spun through an entire 360-degree turn. I fully expected the plane to explode in flames because it still had plenty of fuel aboard. I opened the door and got out faster than lightning! Strike three—*but not out!*

In spite of these three strikes, I still fly my Piper Cub airplane.

When I recall the various near-disasters from which I have been spared, I am tempted to apply a familiar saying to my experience—"A cat has nine lives"—me, too!

I have also had close shaves with automobiles, but they have not been quite as numerous nor as spectacular as those with airplanes. Even though I have never had an automobile accident or even put a scratch on a car, I did experience a near miss on the ice with a van load of people I was taking up a mountain to go skiing. We were virtually run off the road when an eighteen-wheeler began sliding in front of us. With all the effort and strength I could muster, I was able to control the van enough to avoid colliding with this mega-ton truck, but I slid into the median, did a 180-degree turn, and ended up on the other side of the highway heading in the opposite direction.

Another near miss occurred when I was younger. At age fifteen I discovered the keys were in the pickup that my father and I had built. Just for a little driving practice, I took the truck out onto White Oak Road in Campbell, California. This was a back road near the creek about a quarter of a mile from our house. I was going around a corner at only about thirty-five miles per hour when I hit some newly laid gravel. I went into a ferocious spin, and the end of the truck missed a telephone pole by only a foot. No damage done—except to my pride! I immediately took the pickup straight home and never drove it again without permission.

When I was sixteen, my brother let me use his 1936 Ford Cabriolet convertible to take a girl to Forest Pool, a swimming pool in Santa Cruz in the mountains above Saratoga, California. Rain started pouring down as we drove up into the mountains. I had little experience with any kind of driving, much less on rain-slick roads. The car hydroplaned and went into a spin—luckily toward the mountain and not over the edge—which was more than a one-thousand-foot fall! No damage was done to the car—or the people—but it was clearly a close call and a terrifying experience!

Later in my life I was riding a bike down a hill on a dirt road where there was usually no traffic. But a truck came around a corner, coming toward me in my lane—fast! My only choice was to veer off the road. It did not take long for my brain to conclude that dodging the trees in the woods and going down the hill was a better option than hitting the truck head-on. I could not stop the bike but went sailing over the top of it. My hand was ground full of gravel chunks and took several months to heal. The poor driver was so scared that he stopped his truck and came running down the hill to see if I was all right. He carried me and my bike back to my motor home at a trailer park near Branson, Missouri. My quick reaction prevented my hitting the truck head-on and meeting certain death.

The most traumatic near miss I ever suffered in my entire life occurred when I was twelve years old. Along with three thousand other young Scouts, my thirteen-year-old best friend and I were attending a Scout camp near Santa Rosa, California, on November 6, 1941. This was my friend's first Scout encampment. We shared a little tent about eight feet by six feet with two sleeping bags. He apparently became frightened in the middle of the night and lit a candle. He went back to sleep, and the candle ignited his sleeping bag. My best friend burned to death, but I was spared. There were two miracles: my sleeping bag did not burn, and I found enough air to survive. I have often assumed the tent was not put down properly on my side. Also the wind may have been blowing toward the tent on my side so that air came underneath the slight opening, providing sufficient air for me. As you can imagine, this experience left a profound impression on me. I made a commitment to myself and to my scoutmaster, who was also my best friend's father, that I was going to be an Eagle Scout all my life for both of us. I believe I have fulfilled that promise.

When I share stories about these near catastrophes, people ask me, "What do you think about?" These close calls make me even more aware that God has richly blessed me, and I am very thankful I have escaped virtually unscathed. I am glad to be alive to tell about them.

If I had not already believed in angels, these near calamities would have converted me! I have always believed guardian angels were looking after me and my family because we have never suffered any major disasters. I also have great faith in the Bible's promise in Psalm 91:11: "The Lord will command his angels concerning you, to guard you in all your ways."

Surviving these accidents also makes me think I was spared for a purpose—to make the world a better place. I am fully convinced that I would remain in the self-improvement business if I had all the money in the world—or if I were paid nothing at all. If I had a thousand other choices, I would still want to be doing something to encourage people, to motivate people, to help change their lives for the better.

When I recall and reflect upon these life-threatening incidents, I realize I have been given some extra turns at bat in life. As blessed and fortunate as I have been, obviously I have been given more than three strikes—*and I am still at bat!*

16

MY BROTHER—MY HERO

EVER SINCE I was a young boy, I have looked up to my brother, Carl. I liked the way he took charge; I admired his grades in school; I liked the way he looked; I liked the way he dressed; I liked his friends; I liked the respect he showed toward our sister and our mother.

When I was about eight years old and my brother was eleven, he taught me how to swim. Carl and his friends liked to swim in a creek not far from our house. One area of the creek was dammed up to make a good swimming hole. We had no bathing suits, but that did not keep us from enjoying a terrific time swimming and then drying in the sun like turtles. Not only was I ecstatic about Carl's teaching me to swim, but I also felt unbelievably special because Carl willingly took time away from his buddies to turn his full attention to me—his little brother.

"Boy! I'm so lucky to have a big brother like Carl!" I felt those words from the bottom of my heart then. I still do.

Carl also helped me get a job when I was about eight years old. He and some of his friends worked on a farm, and he went to some lengths to get me a job there. I was so proud that I would be working at the same place as my big brother. Years later Carl worked on a dehydrator on the farm, lifting heavy trays of dried fruit. I remember thinking, "Will I ever be big enough and strong enough to lift the trays and do the hard work that Carl does?"

The first time I can recall being upset with Carl was when he was thirteen and I was ten. He ran around with some boys named Jack, Pete, and Frank. They would go to town and go to the movies—without me. Every ounce of my small boyish body yearned to do everything the big guys did. I remember well the first time they did take me. They seemed so big and grown-up to me, especially when they went into a pool hall and shot pool. I had never seen anyone shoot pool before. Afterward, my brother bought me my first banana split. Just thinking about its cool, smooth, delicious flavors brings back warm memories. That banana split was good enough to make me forget being angry at Carl for the times he did not let me go with him and his buddies.

I always looked up to Carl as my role model and mentor. I counted the days until I would reach twelve years old so I could join the Boy Scouts like Carl. Being in the same Boy Scout troop as Carl added to my excitement. By the time I had become a Tenderfoot Scout and then a Second Class Scout, my brother had earned recognition as the first Eagle Scout in our troop. I determined then that regardless of what the other boys did, I would develop the same confidence and the same willingness to do the work required to reach the same high levels of achievement. I, too, would become an Eagle Scout.

The Hi-Y Club was one organization teenagers in high school especially wanted to belong to. Carl was a member, and I recall asking him questions such as how old you had to be and what grade you had to be in to be eligible for membership. I did not know much about the Hi-Y Club. But I did know that if Carl was a member, I also wanted to join. My brother held a school office, so I set a goal to become a student body officer. I was elected vice president of the student body when I was a junior.

A gasoline-powered washing machine motor put on a bicycle with a direct drive was one of the most ingenious inventions I ever saw. And my brother, Carl, was the inventor! I helped him take care of this magnificent machine, and he let me use it. I remember riding home from a school dance on it. The air was crisp, the moon was out, the sky was clear, and there was not much traffic. I zoomed along, feeling like I owned the world and everything in it.

Carl allowed me to share the exhilaration of an even more impressive experience when he bought a 1936 Ford Cabriolet convertible. One of the greatest memories of my teenage years was when my brother told me I could call that Cabriolet half mine and I could use it when he was not in town if I would wash it and look after it.

When I was behind the wheel of that car, I felt as if I were the only one in the world who had such a fantastic automobile. It was a beauty! I believed everybody's eyes were on that car when I drove by. I always wanted to park in a special place at school where I could be seen getting out of my brother's Cabriolet. I have often wondered if my big brother ever knew how much it meant to me that he would share a teenage boy's most valuable possession—his car—with his little brother.

My brother was also my defender. On one occasion Carl heard some boys were going to beat me up or turn my car on its side because I was dating a girl one of them considered his territory. I was small for my age, only five feet tall. (My teenage growth hormones did not kick in until I was sixteen. But in my sixteenth year they made up for lost time: I grew nine inches in height and gained fifty pounds.) I could never have held my own with them, but Carl fought four of them at one time, stacking them up like cordwood.

His strength was amazing! I could hardly comprehend how anyone could be that strong, but at the same time, I realized that I had never seen anyone as angry as Carl was. I never knew anyone who had a big brother like mine who cared that much.

Carl Meyer and his 1936 Ford Cabriolet

A year or so after that victorious escapade, I was reading an assignment for literature class; it was "The Song of Hiawatha" by the venerable American poet Longfellow. Lines from that famous epic, which recounts heroic deeds, described me and my big brother. The lines have taken on even deeper meaning over the decades:

All your strength is in your union.
All your danger is in discord;
Therefore be at peace henceforward,
And as brothers live together.

Another occasion when my brother acted on my behalf as a defender was extremely emotional. It still is. I was seventeen years old and played on the first string of the varsity basketball team. Our school was playing the championship game, but my dad told me that I had to work that afternoon and could not play in this critical game. I insisted it was a championship game and I must play. His response was that he did not know anything about basketball except that it was a waste of time—and I needed to work.

The coach even came to our house to try to persuade my dad to allow me to play in the game, but my dad made him leave. At the time, Carl had a job driving a large semi truck. When he came through town, he would stay at our house. That evening when he came in and learned about the situation, he told my dad I needed to play in this important game. They ended up in a tussle with my brother holding my dad down. With my dad pinned to the floor, Carl threw me the keys to his car and told me to go to the game.

I must have had a good self-image and the ability to focus on the job at hand because I "shifted gears," went to the game, and was high scorer. After the game I had to shift gears again, go home, and face the consequences of my actions. Driving my brother's 1936 Ford Cabriolet, I made sure two blocks from the house that I had enough speed to coast the rest of the way into the driveway. I hoped by cutting off the engine I could return home undetected, enter the house through the back door, go to bed, and wake up the next morning in a new world—rather than face my dad's fury. To my total amazement my dad never mentioned the incident. But I never have forgotten how my brother made sure I got to play in that championship game. By the way, we won.

My brother's work ethic was one of his many attributes I admired. I saw him work hard, earn money, and help our mother. Our dad traveled in his work of making cabinets and furniture, sharpening lawn mowers, and doing "fix-it" jobs. Dad would send money home. I was inspired and developed a desire to be able to work as I saw my dad and my brother work. I wanted to be able to earn my own money. By his example, my brother encouraged my work ethic as well as other positive qualities during those formative years. Many things my brother did or did not do served as my example:

- I played basketball because my brother played basketball.
- I was in the Hi-Y because my brother was in the Hi-Y.
- I was a Scout because my brother was a Scout.
- I joined the track team because my brother was on the track team.
- I did not play football or baseball because my brother did not play football or baseball.

As teenagers do, Carl and I were joking around one day. We were talking about the fact that we did not go to school after World War II. Instead, we planned to go out and start companies so we could give all the college boys jobs. As we have grown older, we have asked each other's advice and have given each other helpful ideas. We have assisted each other financially. I remember early in our adult years when I asked Carl to let me borrow $10,000 to help jump-start my insurance agency to recruit sales associates. He did not hesitate to lend me the money, and he never complained—I never knew what sacrifices he made to help me. Because he helped me so willingly, I only hoped that one day I would be able to help him. My brother can claim a lot of the credit for anything I have accomplished.

Our parents have passed away—my dad in 1963, my mother in 1969. My brother, sister, and I all took part in caring for our parents in their last ten years. I enjoyed the privilege and honor of being able to help just as I saw my brother helping. One of my major lifelong goals was to grow up and be like my brother—his work ethic, his productivity, his integrity, his honesty, and his fairness.

I love you, brother. Thank you for showing me the way.

17

WORK? YES, I LOVE IT!

DECADES AGO I wrote in my journal some notes about work that later I used to write a speech called "The Joy of Work." That speech earned a first place commendation by the National Speakers Association. It is apparent that my convictions about the *value* of work and my *enthusiasm* for work have been a factor in my success from my youth. My convictions and enthusiasm about work are even stronger today, but I fear that work is fast becoming a lost art. Many people fail to recognize and enjoy the benefits of work:

- Work provides an exciting, satisfying thrill.
- Work polishes silver and gold and refines character.
- Work rows "life's boat" upstream.
- Work weeds the garden and cultivates the mind.
- Work lifts weights and spirits.
- Work overcomes adversity and defeat.

- Work is the breath of life.
- Work is love in action.
- Work mines coal from the earth and uncovers diamonds.
- Work supports the wings that put eagles high in the air.
- Work turns poverty into prosperity.
- Work turns dreams into reality.

The value of work and its contribution to a successful life and worthwhile accomplishments have long been celebrated by philosophers, teachers, poets, writers, and businesspeople everywhere:

> *The first qualification for success in my view is a strong work ethic.*
> —Henry Ford II
>
> *In work is the chance to find yourself.*
> —Joseph Conrad
>
> *Work is life, and good work is good life.*
> —James W. Elliott
>
> *To work is to pray.*
> —St. Augustine

I learned early the far-reaching values and joy of work. My master teacher was my father, who came from Germany, where he worked as an apprentice for four years to become a master cabinetmaker. He made hand-carved bedroom suites that sold for five thousand dollars in the 1920s. He took great pride in his workmanship and enjoyed deep satisfaction in using skills he had worked long and hard to perfect. Along with my father, my brother, sister, and I built our home in California. We drew the plans, mixed the cement by hand, laid the brick, threaded the pipe, installed the electrical wiring, and mixed the colors for the paint. The only person we hired was the man who plastered our house. When we asked our father why we were doing all these things ourselves, he said, "We are doing all of this so we can learn to work, to develop the habit of work, to create by our work, to enjoy work, and to feel the sense of pride that comes from work." When we finished the job, we loved our home and were proud of it. I am thankful my parents taught me the profound exhilaration of work well done.

I feel sorry for many young people today who do not have the opportunities I had for work and for the benefits I learned from it. I worked in the grape vineyards with the transient workers, picked prunes and apricots, worked in a cannery, worked in a dehydrator, dug tree stumps, drove a tractor, and trimmed trees. I also had the experience of buying fruit and selling it on a roadside stand. I had the profitable experience of buying, rebuilding, and selling bicycles. In my youth, working was a necessity—an invaluable one. It prepared me to become an entrepreneur. Young people simply do not have the same opportunity today, and I believe they are missing something very valuable. Part of the fortune I inherited from my parents came as they taught me, at an early age, the importance of filling my life with worthwhile activities and the importance of working to *earn* what I wanted in life.

When I review successes I have enjoyed in the past, I find that the decisive role of work in each one is clear. I have always been willing to give what it takes to succeed.

I have always had the willingness to work by a plan to achieve worthwhile, predetermined goals. My own experience and that of others I have observed over the years convince me that when people set challenging goals and discipline themselves to work toward them, they can accomplish anything they desire. Several years ago when Hei Arita, president of PJM Japan, the SMI associate in that country, received a prestigious production award, he was asked how he was able to accomplish so much. "My success can be explained in three words," he said. "Work, work, work."

I have always had the willingness to work by a plan to achieve worthwhile, predetermined goals. I have also made it a practice to hire people—like Barbara Chesser—who have a strong work ethic. Here, she and I are working on a product development project.

Some years ago I read an article about a woman promoted to the presidency of a motion picture company, Twentieth Century Fox. She began as a model, worked as an actress, and then became involved in production at Paramount Studios. As a result of excellent work on two high-paying pictures, she earned her appointment as president of Twentieth Century Fox at a salary exceeding a quarter of a million dollars per year.

When this successful young woman was interviewed for the article, she was asked if she felt proud to be the first woman to become president of a major motion picture company. She replied that she would much rather people note that her success was the logical outcome of her hard work to meet the goals and achieve the objectives she had set for herself.

Her attitude toward the significant role work played in her success reminds me of some down-to-earth wisdom my mother used to say to me:

Sitting there wishing
Makes no person great.
The Lord sends the fishes,
But **you** *must dig the bait!*

I have noted that sometimes our business can create an *illusion*, an *aura*, or a sense of *euphoria* that causes people to overlook the need for good hard work. They take a look at our positive material; they associate with positive people in our business; they attend meetings with positive emphasis. Then they go home excited, feeling good, *expecting* great things to happen.

Some of these people immediately set to work as hard as they can and make things happen. They expect success, and they work for it. Other people, however, look at our positive materials, meet the positive people, sit in the positive meetings, and go home feeling good about the business—but then just sit down and *wait* for positive results to happen automatically. They overlook entirely the need for good hard work. They never realize that "There ain't no such thing as a free lunch." They soon disappear from the business.

What my parents taught me has, year by year, taken on an even fuller, richer meaning as I have experienced the wonderful world of work. I see many things more clearly.

Work allows people to use their full potential for creative expression. On a trip with one of my sons to South Texas to visit my brother, Carl, I enjoyed seeing my brother's face and watching his eyes sparkle as he described several of his new inventions and his futuristic plans in his field. It was *artistry and poetry put to music*, a man in love with his work, his electric lightbulb, his cotton gin, the products of his creativity, his masterpieces. My son and I were completely mesmerized as Carl talked about the technology of an air shield he had designed to go on a car. Carl was obviously *a man in love with his work*. He was like Edison—working in his laboratory, losing all sense of time, and frequently forgetting mealtime because he loved his work so intensely.

Work fills time with intensely interesting and satisfying activities. I meet many people who are not happy in their careers, but they keep on plodding in the same old jobs, spending a lifetime *marking time*, *hanging on*, or *waiting for retirement*. People who do not possess a passion for their work should get out and pursue some other career. I firmly believe that people need to find work that utilizes their unique potential and inspires in them an engaging intensity. Truer words were never spoken than those by Carlyle, the English essayist, "Blessed is he who has found his work; let him ask no other blessedness."

Work gives people an opportunity to share something of themselves with other people. "By your fruits you shall know them" refers to spiritual things, but it applies just as truly to all realms of life. My greatest satisfaction is pursuing work that helps improve the lives of other people—that is, "motivating people to their full potential."® Words from Albert Schweitzer capture my philosophy about work choices; he said that whatever work people choose to pursue, they should make sure it is of service to other people because that provides the most longstanding satisfaction.

Work increases energy and the capacity to perform. If you have ever tried to jog, you find that when you first begin you are unable to run far before you feel exhausted. If you give up at this level, you will never set any records. You can either quit, or you can keep on in spite of the fatigue. Then you experience what is known as "second wind." Suddenly there is a new source, a new reservoir of strength and stamina, a new capacity for exertion.

The principle of "second wind" works in business just as it does in sports or any other activity. When you get caught up in an exciting spirit of competition, you suddenly find that it is no harder to complete four or five major actions in a day than you had previously thought it was to do three. With persistent performance at the new level, pushing against the newly attained record, you establish the new level as a habit and are ready to move to even higher accomplishments in your work. Successful work increases energy and builds greater capacity, which enables people to perform at higher levels of efficiency and achievement.

Work increases desire. A good friend in Waco, Texas, Kurt Kaiser, a world-famous composer and pianist, gave me the best example of this principle I know. He said that the greatest composers do not just sit down and write because they are inspired, but they are inspired because they work. Many people have it all backwards; they want to sit around and wait to be inspired before they do something worthwhile. It simply does not work that way. When people get to work on a worthwhile project, inspiration follows. Thomas Edison said it well, "Success is 2 percent inspiration and 98 percent perspiration."

Work brings desired rewards. Nothing is more satisfying to me than a job well done. I have never thought of work as punishment because I knew that kind of thinking would never motivate me to achieve my goals. Working hard does have some drawbacks; it occasionally brings difficult and painful moments. There have been times when I wanted to chuck the whole thing. But my experience has been that for every drawback, there is a greater benefit or desirable reward.

One of the most outstanding rewards of work is simply the satisfaction of having completed a worthwhile goal and earning the rewards the completed goal brings. Tolstoy, the renowned Russian author and philosopher, offered keen insight into work when he said, "The more that is given, the less the people will work for themselves." For me, hard work has been the way to discover the end of many rainbows.

My mother knew a great deal of poetry by heart and often quoted her favorite lines. One stanza she recited to me countless times during my youth is now one of my favorites:

The heights by great men reached and kept
Were not attained by sudden flight,
But they, while their companions slept,
Were toiling upward in the night.

18

MY LOVE AFFAIR WITH A CAMERA

MY LOVE AFFAIR *with a camera* began when I was a kid. My mother took pictures of everything. I knew she enjoyed pictures immensely because she was always showing ones taken a month, a year, and several years before. My mother's parents also had a camera and used it for taking countless pictures. We were one of the few fortunate families with pictures taken before the turn of the century (all the way back to 1890 and in each generation since).

When I was sixteen, I broke the existing record of picking prunes in California. I knew I was going to break the record—I had set that as my goal. To get an early start, I hung flashlights in the trees where I was working to accomplish my goal of 101 boxes of prunes. I had the owner of the prune orchard to take my picture, and it appeared in the local newspaper. This hard-earned accomplishment tremendously strengthened *my love affair with a camera.*

I took many rolls of film while in the military. I still have most of those treasured pictures—pictures of paratroopers jumping out of airplanes, pictures of airplanes, pictures of crews, pictures taken from the air while floating down to land, and pictures after

Working a sixteen-hour day on August 1, 1944, I set the record—picking 101 boxes of prunes.

I hit the ground. As the only one in the entire company who owned a camera, I was asked by many others to take their pictures. I made many friends then with my camera—and still do.

When the first Polaroid camera came out in 1948, I was in the life insurance business. It dawned on me that the Polaroid would be an incredible prospecting tool if used properly. One of the ways I put the camera to good use was going to a neighborhood after school and taking Polaroid pictures of children playing. After the sixty seconds required for the film to develop, I would go up to the house, knock on the door, and give the picture to the children's mother, father, or whoever came to the door. I would say, "I saw your kids out there, and they looked so beautiful I just couldn't help but take this picture. I thought you might like to have it." Usually they would be overwhelmed because they generally did not have a camera and often had not seen or even heard of a Polaroid camera. In addition, they were astonished that a stranger would do what I had done. Next, I would give them my card and explain to them what I did in my business and ask them if I could stop by sometime and talk to them about a program or some good ideas I had for the family. If I was talking to the mother, she would generally say something like, "Let me talk to my husband, and we will give you a call." I must have made as many as one hundred appointments a year just from the use of my camera.

I did the same thing with businesses. I would go through a businessplace, taking four or five pictures. Then I would go in and give them to the person in charge as a way of introducing myself. As you can imagine, the pictures opened up numerous business opportunities.

Over the years I have used the camera for many, many purposes. Photography has served numerous business objectives as well as being an interesting hobby. For example, I have invested extensively in real estate. When I look at real estate, I take two or three rolls of film of a property that interests me. I set up a file and keep it for years. Having the pictures on file has been an incredibly valuable resource. A similar use is taking pictures of construction ideas to keep on file for use when I remodel or construct a new building.

Landscape pictures have always been a favorite subject. I have taken pictures all over the world and have a large master book of them. I have reproduced several hundred landscapes into large two and a half by three feet pictures. They are matted, framed, and fully identified with a plaque. Many of these are displayed in our corporate headquarters offices in Waco, Texas. These large landscape pictures are also one of the major gifts I enjoy giving to friends.

Jane and I own a large thoroughbred horse farm on Salado Creek, about forty or fifty miles from our Waco home. When we first bought the farm, I did not know much about the horse business. So I took my camera to Kentucky and visited a half dozen of the finest thoroughbred horse farms and facilities in the world, such as Calumet. I took pictures of every single part of every facility—the metal doors and how they slide, the feeding troughs, the fences, the roof, the drainage system, the type of brick work, the concrete work, and even the cupola and the weather vane on top of stable buildings. When I returned to Waco, I made a three-ring binder with a different tab for all the various components or features. Without an architect but by using the pictures I had taken, a local carpenter was able to build our stallion barn and other facilities. People from all over the country say we have the finest thoroughbred horse facility they have ever seen.

On another occasion I wanted to start a particular kind of manufacturing company but did not know the kind of equipment to purchase. I asked an out-of-state company, "Do you mind if I take pictures of all of your equipment and the layout and talk to some of your people?" The response was, "Not at all." With a notebook and camera, in fewer than four hours I had all the information—such as the names of the equipment—I needed to start my company. My camera saved me a great deal of both time and money.

My *love affair with a camera* was romanced by an unusual chair in Palm Springs, California, and provided an idea for some unique chairs in our home. When Jane and I were in Palm

Springs on a business trip, we saw a very unusual chair. We liked the general features of the chair, but it incorporated into the back of the chair an animal we did not particularly care for. Also, the chair was extraordinarily expensive. But we did like the concept carried out in the chair. We took a picture of it and showed it to a cabinetmaker in Waco. We bought a chair from an unpainted furniture store, took the back off, and the cabinetmaker replaced it with the design of a fish drawn by an artist from a nearby university. Now we have half a dozen of what we call our "fish chairs." We produced these unique, attractive chairs for approximately 15 percent of the cost of the one we saw in California. My trusty camera made all of this possible.

I believe the familiar saying, "A picture is worth a thousand words," is literally true. It certainly was accurate in my landscaping work. I was having difficulty communicating to my yard man how I wanted my plants trimmed. With my camera in hand, I drove around town taking pictures of how I wanted about twenty different kinds of plants to look. I put these pictures in an album and gave them to my yard man. I never said a word, and I have not said anything to him about them since that time. But we enjoy a beautiful yard based on these pictures.

> "A picture is worth a thousand words."

Another satisfying use of my camera is with our Christmas decorations. Because one of Jane's hobbies is Christmas decorations, we have two hundred or more different types. I gave her an album of pictures of all these decorations taken in the locations she liked best for each one. Every year now she refers to her picture album to know exactly where in our home to put each of the beautiful Christmas decorations.

Collecting antique cars is one of my hobbies, and my camera comes in handy with it. Prospective buyers I talk to say they have never bought a car without seeing it firsthand. Yet all of the sales I have made of antique cars are over the telephone because I provide prospective buyers with a set of twenty different pictures taken of the car inside and out, underneath, the front, the back, the side—every single detail.

Negatives and some of the pictures from over five thousand rolls of film are filed by the year and by the month. I still take about three hundred to five hundred rolls per year and add to this collection. From it I made a picture album to give to each of my children of our family history and genealogy. My family treasures these pictures more than any other material present we could possibly give them.

Stronger today than ever, *my love affair with a camera* has never required sophisticated equipment like professional photographers use. I started with a plain, ordinary camera and still use a no-frills, pocket-held, self-focusing camera. I always wanted to keep it simple.

19

FLYING MY PIPER CUB

EACH PERSON is special, with unique potential and with unique ways of tapping and using that potential. Case in point: Flying my Piper Cub is a fairly unique, untraditional, unorthodox method I use to tap my potential and reach goals in every area of life—Family and Home, Financial and Career, Mental and Educational, Physical and Health, Social and Cultural, and Spiritual and Ethical.

Take, for example, the Financial and Career area of my life. I am now at the point in this area of life where I have turned over to others the CEO responsibilities of many of the companies in Meyer Family Enterprises. One of my goals is to empower and mentor these executives. When I am flying my Piper Cub, I do some of my best thinking about constructive ways to mentor these individuals. In addition, one of the executives sometimes accompanies me, and we have excellent discussions about how to handle certain aspects of the company that person is responsible for. At other times, the best mentoring is simply leaving the executives alone and letting them handle, lead, and manage their companies. While I am flying my Piper Cub, they are taking complete charge of their company.

Flying my Piper Cub is one unique way I use my particular strengths and express my unique interests to reach certain goals I have set in each area of my life.

Central Texas is blessed with beautiful weather most of the year. The agreeable Texas weather provides many opportunities for me to fly my little Piper Cub. The spring is particularly enjoyable because in Texas everything is green and beautiful with flowers and trees in bloom everywhere. Taking advantage of nature's beauty enhances every area of my life. It especially bolsters my mental health, which in turn also supports my physical health.

Spending time with individual members of my family is a high priority with me. Flying my Piper Cub enables me to visit with my adult children and grandchildren more frequently. For instance, I enjoy flying to the new country home of my youngest son, Billy. His home is approximately fifteen miles from the Waco airport. The driveway up to Billy's home is about a half mile long. Billy made a grass landing strip alongside the road. I land my plane parallel to the road and taxi right up to Billy's house or to a nearby lake. This arrangement makes it easy for me to visit Billy and his wife Deborah, their son Adam, and daughter Christen.

Billy has a lake about the size of two city blocks that he stocks with fish. From that lake, Adam recently caught one of the largest bass ever caught in our entire county. It weighed twelve pounds—an amazing feat! We do not keep the fish we catch, but put them back into the lake so others can enjoy catching them. Billy also has horses, and Adam competes in calf-roping contests, which he is very good at. Flying my Piper Cub to Billy's home in the country enables me to enjoy more of his family life.

My son Larry also owns a farm in the country; it is about forty miles from Waco. He drives there once or twice a week to fish and to check on his animals. He raises deer and exotic game animals. Larry has also cleared a place on his farm where I can land my Piper Cub. I enjoy visiting with all Larry's family on that farm—his wife Lynn and their three children, Jessica, Jennifer, and Josh.

I sometimes enjoy flying my Piper Cub without a definite destination in mind. I have landed on more than one hundred grass strips within a two-hundred-mile range of Waco, Texas. Having uninterrupted time to think about my life and my priorities helps me keep my life in order and well balanced. In addition, I never know which area of my life may be serendipitously enriched. I have made a lot of new friends flying like this. Recently, I landed on a grass strip where an elderly gentleman ran out to greet me. His hobby is restoring airplanes; he restored the first mail plane flown in Texas—a beautiful job! He has also restored a World War I plane; he said it took him seven years to restore it. He and I spent about an hour together as he filled me in on some interesting Texas history and some intriguing information about the fine art of airplane restoration.

Sometimes when I am flying my Piper Cub, I fly without having any particular direction. When sightseeing, I have come across the unusual. In fact, the very, very unusual. A couple of years ago I was flying sixty miles north of Waco and saw a grass landing strip right alongside of some buildings that were obviously out in the country.

I enjoy banking at the Cow Pasture Bank.

After landing, I heard somebody holler, "Hey, Mister, would you like to have some cookies?" I looked up and noticed a sign that said "Cow Pasture Bank."

To my amazement, it was a fly-in bank fifty miles away from a town of any size. I asked an employee, "Do you have much money in this bank?" She answered, "Yes, several hundred million." I was astonished! My next question was, "Where do you get all your customers?" She replied, "Several thousand fly-ins like yourself."

I was so intrigued that I went inside the bank building. The decorations consisted of barbed wire, country farm relics, and pictures of cattle drives. The wonderful aroma of fresh-baked cookies filled the place! I found out they bake one hundred dozen cookies every day. Right then and there, I opened up a bank account at this unusual bank. I have thoroughly enjoyed sending people checks from the Cow Pasture Bank.

By the way, the cookies were great!

When I fly to Summers Mill Farm, which is about fifty miles from Waco, I also land on a grass landing strip. I call ahead and have an antique pickup there for me to drive—a 1942 Ford (the same vintage as my Piper Cub) or a 1940 Chevrolet. My business interests require fairly frequent trips there. For example, I own the largest ostrich farm in the Southwest. Not only do I enjoy flying my Piper Cub to Summers Mill Farm, but I also save a great deal of time by flying rather than driving.

I subscribe to the *Piper Cub Magazine*. This publication has quickly become one of my favorites. It includes informative articles about the Piper Cub and other Piper Cub owners like myself. It also describes activities of the Piper Cub Club, like the Piper Cub "fly-ins" where Piper Cub owners eat breakfast together and swap amusing stories. These fly-ins provide great relaxation and even greater socializing with colorful and distinctive individuals! In addition, I have met some very astute businesspeople and, as a result, made several profitable business transactions!

To tell you just a little more about my Piper Cub—it is a tail-dragger as opposed to the tricycle gear used on modern airplanes. My Piper Cub is the kind of airplane most people trained in during the forties. The Piper Cub has a front seat for the pilot and a seat behind the pilot for a passenger. It is capable of flying at a maximum speed of 120 miles per hour, but most often I fly about ninety miles per hour. I generally stay close to the ground—about a thousand feet—so I can sightsee.

I feel rejuvenated—almost like a young kid again—when I am flying my Piper Cub. I can turn left, or I can turn right. I can fly up, or I can fly down. I learned to fly when I was in my early twenties and have done a lot of flying since then. I have made 1,750 landings in my plane in the last five years alone. I fly an average of once a week, or more than fifty times a year, for recreation, relaxation, or mentally reviewing business ideas.

By no stretch of the imagination, flying my Piper Cub enriches all areas of my life—even the Spiritual and Ethical area, for when I am flying in and out of clouds or simply seeing the beautiful country below, I sing, I quote poetry, I think of my friends, and I think of how my Creator has blessed me so richly! The poem "High Flight" captures the feelings I experience when flying my Piper Cub:

Oh, I have slipped the surly bonds of earth
And danced the skies on laughter-silvered wings;
Sunward I've climbed, and joined the tumbling mirth
Of sun-split clouds—and done a hundred things
You have not dreamed of—wheeled and soared and swung
High in the sunlit silence. Hov'ring there
I've chased the shouting wind along, and flung
My eager craft through footless halls of air.
Up, up the long, delirious, burning blue
I've topped the windswept heights with easy grace

Where never lark, or even eagle flew.
And, while with silent, lifting mind I've trod
The high untrespassed sanctity of space,
Put out my hand, and touched the face of God.

20

A SPECIAL CELEBRATION

EACH OF MY CHILDREN is very special to me, and I have tried to communicate that clearly and consistently to all five of them. It has been easier at times for me to send that message in writing rather than only verbally. When our youngest daughter, Leslie, turned twenty-one, I felt a wonderful and overwhelming attitude of *joy*. So I sent her a letter called *The Top 21 Joys of My Life* as she celebrated her twenty-first birthday.

1. The joy of being present when you were born—a beautiful, screaming baby.
2. The joy of holding you as a baby and at eighteen months having you stand in my hand.
3. The joy of pulling you around the block on Mount Rockwood Circle in your little red wagon at ages two, three, and four.
4. The joy of seeing you and your friend Kimberly riding around and around in our driveway in the early eighties in your own little red two-seater car.

5. The joy of dancing with you under the stars in Acapulco in the late seventies.
6. The joy we all shared together on our first trip to the Caymans in 1979 when we jumped ship.
7. The joy of listening to you and your cousins, Mike and Brady, laughing while skiing out of control downhill in Snowmass in the early 1980s.
8. The joy of watching you all through the 1980s, day after day, on the floor in the den flip-flopping a towel back and forth, playing with our family dog, Fonzie, and later, Magnum.
9. The joy of witnessing you accept Jesus Christ as your personal Savior.
10. The joy of being with you and seeing your excitement upon finding a little spider fifty feet deep at the bottom of the ocean during our underwater photography course in 1984—a very special father-daughter time.

Both of our daughters—Leslie and Janna—are special joys. Of Janna, Leslie says, "First my sister, forever my friend."

11. The joy of seeing you light up as you met two presidents of the United States—Ronald Reagan and later, George Bush.

12. The joy of a very, very special time for Thanksgiving in 1989 with the four of us—your sister Janna, your mother, you, and me—skiing, playing games, sharing, and talking about the future.
13. The joy of Christmas week in Aspen with most of our family in 1990 and the week following with Carl, Carol, Sis, Uncle Bill, and Bettye—and the evening in the railroad car laughing and laughing as we listened to Carol recite stories about her dog.
14. The joy of seeing you turn sixteen and getting your first car—a Jeep Cherokee filled with balloons.
15. The joy of seeing you enjoying the Caymans with your girlfriends for the past fifteen years.
16. The joy of seeing you a hundred times sitting on the kitchen counter talking, sharing, and laughing with Janna and your mother.
17. The joy of going to all of the Waco Christian School ballgames and seeing you cheerlead.
18. The joy of seeing your eyes as you beheld the splendor of some of the great sights in the world such as the Great Wall of China; the Coliseum in Rome; the Opera House in Sydney, Australia; the Peace Memorial in Hiroshima, Japan; and the Pearl Harbor Memorial in Hawaii.
19. The joy of having the great honor of presenting your graduation diploma to you from Waco Christian School in 1992.
20. The joy of watching you in your role as Aunt Leslie to Morgan, Brooke, and Kelsey.
21. And perhaps the greatest joy of all, at this time in your life, is seeing you develop character, personality, and a sweet spirit like that of your grandmother (my mother) and your mother.

21

MY MOST MEMORABLE INTERVIEW

I HAVE ENJOYED my profession as much as anyone else ever has. My career in selling, marketing, and business has been pleasant, uplifting, and at times exhilarating. My positive attitude, love for people, and commitment to help them use more of their potential make getting up and going to work each day fun. Because I have worked hard and been blessed with success, I have enjoyed many opportunities to be interviewed in the United States and internationally on radio and television and in newspapers and business journals. I remember granting as many as sixty interviews and press conferences some months.

Some interviews were very unusual. The most memorable interview I ever had was in 1977 with Mitsuko Shimomura, considered one of the top female journalists in the world. She worked for prestigious publications in Asia including the *Asahi Evening News*, which enjoyed the largest daily circulation in the world at that time. She has conducted interviews with top executives all over the world and has written several books about these interviews.

Underlying all her questions about multinational corporations and their principles, their procedures, and their roles in the world ran a continuing concern for people—for the welfare of the individual. All those she interviewed expressed their recognition of the need to use the full potential of individuals—in every facet of business. But she pointed out that it was in the interview with me that she had found one executive who had built an entire business to help people use their potential to achieve their own personal goals—a business dedicated to "motivating people to their full potential."®

Since only ten executives were featured in the book, each interview was quite comprehensive. Here are excerpts of the interview between Shimomura and me:

SHIMOMURA: Mr. Meyer, among all the people I've interviewed, you're the only one who has been able to express his philosophy of living in a single sentence. I believe I'm quoting you correctly when I say, "Whatever you vividly imagine, ardently desire, sincerely believe, and enthusiastically act upon, must inevitably come to pass." How long have you lived by this principle?

MEYER: Ever since I was a youngster. My mother taught me you can accomplish anything if you believe strongly enough in yourself. Self-motivation is the key to successful living.

SHIMOMURA: How about education? Isn't that also necessary?

MEYER: Only relatively so beyond high school. Everyone needs basic skills. From that point on, those who desire specialized education—engineering, medicine, law, etc.—should

This is the cover of the book (obviously in Japanese!) Mitsuko Shimomura wrote about several American business people, including me.

pursue it. Others can achieve success in the field of their choice with self-motivation. Formal classwork is not *necessarily* the only key to success.

SHIMOMURA: Do you believe each person is responsible for his or her own success or failure?

MEYER: Definitely! When people apply the law of cause and effect, they don't make the same mistake twice—they learn from their mistakes. Thus, they educate themselves and learn to succeed.

SHIMOMURA: Is that all there is to it—profiting from mistakes?

MEYER: No. The principle reason for failure is *thinking* failure. People can change their *way of life* only when they change their *way of thinking*.

SHIMOMURA: Do you mean even I could become fantastically successful just by *thinking* success?

MEYER: You certainly could, providing you matched those *thoughts* with the necessary *actions*.

SHIMOMURA: Haven't you *ever* failed?

MEYER: Of course. I became a millionaire at age twenty-seven—and I was flat broke at twenty-eight. But I learn from my mistakes, and I don't make the same mistakes again. That's part of my continuing education.

SHIMOMURA: Implementing a successful frame of mind with action—is that the secret of success?

MEYER: To be totally correct, the secret of success is goal setting. One who is a failure sets a goal to fail. The successful person sets *goals of achievement*—implemented with a successful frame of mind and action.

SHIMOMURA: I understand you began your career as an insurance salesman. Is that correct?

MEYER: I was about nineteen when I decided there was an opportunity for me in the insurance business. I applied to almost forty companies, but they all turned me down because I was too young and lacked experience. Finally one hired me, but I lost the job three weeks later. They told me it was because I was too shy to approach strangers, I had a speech impediment (stuttering), and I hadn't graduated from college.

SHIMOMURA: What did you do?

MEYER: Anger was my first reaction, but then I remembered my mother's encouragement—that I could accomplish *anything* as long as I believed in myself. So I opened the office door of my former employer and said an exit line worthy of the finest movie actor: "You are losing the number one insurance salesman in America. The day will come when I'll break every sales record in the country. You'll read about it in the newspapers!" Then I slammed the door and left.

SHIMOMURA: I understand you *did* break a record.

MEYER: I certainly did. During the next year I established a sales record that has yet to be surpassed.

SHIMOMURA: And you became a millionaire?

MEYER: Correct.

SHIMOMURA: With that kind of success in selling insurance, why did you leave it to found Success Motivation Institute?

MEYER: First, because I realized I had far more potential for success than I was using. Second, because the sales volume of the other salesmen increased when they used the techniques I had explained to them. That's why I decided to launch SMI—to share with others *proven* methods for using more of their potential to successfully reach their goals.

SHIMOMURA: How does a person determine "potential for success"?

MEYER: When people want to discover their untapped potential for accomplishing something better, they must first remove thought patterns and habits restricting their success. Once they are mentally free of such conditioning, they can set new goals and develop a plan of action to achieve them.

SHIMOMURA: Can you explain the contents of an SMI program?

MEYER: Every SMI program is built around its Plan of Action. This is the all-important feature that makes the program workable because it stresses clarification—the necessity for *writing* each goal and the details of how and when it will be accomplished.

SHIMOMURA: Why do you emphasize "writing"?

MEYER: Many of us have dreams or half-formed visions, but they don't become *real* to us until we see them in our own handwriting. "Writing" clarifies our thinking. Crystallized thoughts enable us to prioritize our goals and to write out the action steps we must take to reach each goal.

SHIMOMURA: Mr. Meyer, you emphasized how "success" means different things to different people. Success isn't necessarily confined to money, power, and material possessions.

MEYER: That's right. Personal success is a matter of personal definition. Success for one person may be the overcoming of a physical or social handicap—for another, it may be the discovery of a new personal talent. Of course, it can also be the accumulation of wealth.

SHIMOMURA: I notice you always put "making money" as the last on any list of human accomplishments. Don't you consider money important?

MEYER: Of course, I do. But the ability to make money—accumulate wealth—is a *result* of becoming successful, not the entirety of success itself. There are more important aims and accomplishments than simply making money. Each self-motivation and goal-setting program teaches how to set goals in all areas of life—Family and Home, Financial and Career, Mental and Educational, Physical and Health, Social and Cultural, and Spiritual and Ethical. When one sets personal goals in each area of life, crystallizes desire, sets target dates for achievement, and puts desire into practice with confidence and enthusiasm, ignoring critics, success is bound to follow.

SHIMOMURA: Emphasizing six areas of life shows your intention is to help broaden and deepen life.

MEYER: I call it the "Total Person" concept. Attaining contentment, satisfaction, and happiness cannot be accomplished by concentrating on only *one* or *two* areas of life. A balanced approach to life is the most effective way to achieve contentment and happiness—or to sum it up, success. That is the Total Person approach.

SHIMOMURA: Then one who concentrates solely on becoming wealthy—at the expense of every other human factor—is *not* a Total Person.

MEYER: That's true.

SHIMOMURA: Judging from everything I know about you, *you've* set high goals to become a Total Person. One of them must have been the accumulation of money.

MEYER: It was and is—but money certainly isn't the most important goal to me.

SHIMOMURA: That idea is directly opposed by some of the successful men I've interviewed. They say money buys power, and power in the hands of an intelligent person can accomplish a lot of good.

MEYER: That depends on your definition of "good." Personally, I feel that I'm a temporary custodian of whatever wealth I may have. It's my responsibility to use it as wisely as possible. I know I can't take it with me.

SHIMOMURA: Then profits can be flawed?

MEYER: Certainly. There are examples of this happening everywhere all over the world. I know that one of my companies turned down an unscrupulous offer just a few years ago. By refusing to compromise our business principles, we provided validity for the Total Person concept. Financial profit at the expense of the other aspects of life is worthless.

SHIMOMURA: What *personal* goals have you set for your own life?

MEYER: The goal for my original company was to "motivate people to their full potential."® That is still the goal I hold steadfastly to for my companies around the world.

SHIMOMURA: What do you think about the future?

MEYER: I'm extremely optimistic. There has never been a time in the history of the world when young people were more creative, original, and enthusiastic. People are our greatest resource.

SHIMOMURA: Mr. Meyer, there is one final question I would like to ask. What is your definition of "happiness"?

MEYER: *Happiness*, like *success*, means different things to different people. I can only tell you what it means to me. Happiness is contentment, security, love, and the knowledge that I have made a meaningful contribution to my day and time, that I have made use of my unlimited potential and shared it with others.

22

BARTERING FOR BUSINESS

WHEN I WAS A CHILD, I watched people trade "this for that," and they called it *bartering*. I noticed that people who had apricots traded them with people who had corn. Others who raised strawberries traded them for artichokes. Others who grew nut trees, like walnuts, traded shelled walnuts for either canned fruit or so many months of vegetables. I saw people trade services—cleaning, painting, plumbing—every kind of service you can imagine—for products and produce. I saw people help paint someone's house in exchange for getting their car engine overhauled. All this was during my formative and impressionable years, right after the Great Depression. I was between eight and fourteen years old at the time.

I evidently learned the lessons well because I immediately applied the same principle when I began selling insurance. In addition, I have used it with other products and services I have sold over the past fifty years. Here are some of my most memorable bartering experiences.

On an insurance selling trip to Dalton, Georgia, I stopped at a grocery store, talked to the owner, and made a presentation to him about a particular type of insurance contract. The owner liked it very much but said he did not have any money. My immediate response was, "Who said anything about *money*?" We were talking about a premium of between $250 and $500. I ended up trading him the first year's premium for half a cow. Making the sale and bartering for the cow was easy. The big challenge was, "What am I going to do with half of a cow in the trunk of my car, eighteen miles from home, and no freezer?" I knew I must do something quickly. I went to an appliance store in nearby Columbus, Georgia, and made an insurance presentation to the owner, Mr. Starnes. I sold him a life insurance policy and then traded him a freezer for the first year's premium. I did have to use some cash to get a butcher to cut up the half a cow, wrap the individual pieces, and mark them so I could put them in the freezer.

This picture was taken of me in 1948 as I was leaving my apartment for a day of selling or bartering for business.

On many other occasions while selling insurance out in the country, I have traded insurance premiums for vegetables, chickens, cleaning, and laundry. One of my favorite memories is of sitting in my car in the rain in front of Baker Village High

School with M. C. Weatherington, trying to recruit him as a sales associate. His initial response was, "It seems very difficult to sell." I asked him, "If we could go into the TV store right across the street from the school and I could either sell a policy or trade it for a TV, would you come to work for me and this company?" He answered, "Yes." So we went into the Baker Village TV store, sold the owner an insurance policy, and traded the premium for a television set. Mr. Weatherington went to work for me that day! He still lives in Valdosta, Georgia, and he is still in the life insurance business with the same company after more than forty-five years!

Probably the most extraordinary trade I have ever heard of being made, at least by an insurance salesman, was in Fort Lauderdale, Florida, around 1954. I was working with Bill Armor, who has been a dear friend for a lifetime. He and I were in our twenties and working with positively no inhibitions. Our biggest assets were excitement, enthusiasm, and energy. The thrill of the chase compelled us—the excitement of getting up each day to go out and make a sale, the boundless enthusiasm for what we were doing, and the unlimited energy to do it! We made an early start that day and called on Mr. and Mrs. Wynn Castille, who owned a hotel near the beach in Fort Lauderdale. After we made our life insurance presentation, Wynn Castille said, "I would love to buy that policy, but right now I have a bigger problem." I asked what the problem was. He said, "I need to be able to borrow some money on this hotel because I want to do a housing development, and the bank will loan only 50 percent of the appraised value on the hotel."

I thought for a minute and said, "It's a shame it's not a life insurance policy because if it were a life insurance policy, you could borrow 95 percent on it. It sounds kind of wild, but a thought just occurred to me. Why don't you swap the hotel to us for an insurance policy, take the insurance policy to the bank, borrow 95 percent, and go do your deal?"

Anyway, we did—and he did! He borrowed the money at the Pan American Bank in Miami, Florida, from a bank officer by the name of George Farner. He built his subdivision, and he remained one of Bill Armor's close personal friends until he died. That was the largest single-premium policy that had ever been sold by anyone in South Florida at the time.

Once Bill Armor and I got a taste of helping meet people's needs—and ours—and once we had experienced the euphoria of making a deal, we began to look for other ways to be different and unique in both packaging and marketing our products. One that is not quite as dramatic but is certainly unique is our trading for a yacht. Then the company, after getting the yacht, asked if we would help them sell it. We said, "Of course." Next we thought, "Who buys yachts? Rich people buy yachts! Where are the rich people?" They are either over on Miami Beach, or they are coming into the airport on their private planes. So I said, "Why don't we drive out to the airport where the private planes land and use Bill Armor's Cadillac as a limousine and offer a free ride to anyone who lands there. This would give us a chance to talk with a good prospect."

Before we had been at the airport two hours, we met Denise Darcel, the movie star, and a group of her friends. They accepted our offer of a ride, and on the way to the hotel we took them by to show them the yacht, *Souris*. The result was we made a sale of the yacht; that is, we got a down payment of 20 percent, with the balance to be paid over five months. Denise Darcel had one party on it and never made another payment. We repossessed the yacht.

In a few weeks we followed that plan again and sold the yacht to an individual from Boston in exchange for some stock.

He paid us 20 percent down in the form of stock in his company, and like the first sale, he did not make any other payments. He said he did not want to go through with the deal because it cost too much to operate the yacht. This made two sales of the yacht *Souris* in less than thirty days. However, we had collected 20 percent down on each sale.

I remember Captain Frank Boehm's comments about the eighty-two foot yacht. "Mr. Meyer, this has to be one of your better businesses, selling this yacht every other week and getting it back."

The sale of this yacht—and the resale . . . and the resale—probably brought the most fun I ever had making a sale.

The third time was a charm! Bill Armor and I were driving around selling insurance when a young man drove by us in a brand-new yellow Cadillac with a black top. We followed him across the causeway to Miami. Near this causeway are several islands with luxurious homes—all on the water. Our young prospect in the yellow Cadillac turned onto one of the islands, and we followed him. He then turned into a palatial home. When he got out of his car, he said, "Why are you following me?" We asked him if he had a yacht behind his home on the waterway. He said he did not, so we told him about the yacht *Souris*. Then he told us he was from Metagine, Colombia, and his name was J. B. Londomo. We showed him the yacht that day and made a sale—this time all for cash but in Colombian pesos, and the money was put in the Pan American Bank in Miami, Florida.

Recently I had a motorcoach for sale. I advertised it in the *Family Motorcoach Magazine*, and I received many responses. One of them was from a man in California who had a home in Palm Springs. We traded the motorcoach for the home on the golf course in Palm Springs. He is very happy with the trade, and we are very happy with the trade!

In April 1996, I was at our home in Palm Springs and needed a car for everyday use. I placed an ad in an antique car publication for one of my 1936 Fords in hopes of making a trade for a newer car. A man in Nebraska answered the ad but said he did not know if he had enough money to buy the car. I asked, "Do you have anything you would like to trade?" He said, "Yes, I have a brand-new Cadillac—a Seville SLS with a Northstar engine, and it has one thousand miles on it." I told him I would send him pictures of the 1936 Ford and see if we could "make a trade." When he received the pictures of the 1936 Ford Phaeton and a spec sheet, he called me on the phone. He said, "Let's trade even." I replied, "It's a done deal." When he got the 1936 Ford Phaeton, I called him. He was very satisfied with the trade. When I got the Cadillac out in Palm Springs, I was also very satisfied.

Another time back in earlier years I was looking at a choice lot in an exclusive residential area in Columbus, Georgia, where I wanted to live. The man who owned the lot was W. G. Salter. He told me how much he wanted for it. I said, "Well, I could pay you that, but is there something you want done that I have the skill to do so we could make a trade?" He replied, "Yes, I have several homes I have been trying to sell. I am in the construction business as well as the tire business. I have been unable to sell these homes." I asked him, "If I sell the homes, do I get a title to the lot?" His reply was, "Yes." Within a forty-five day period I had sold all of the homes to people I knew in Columbus, Georgia. I earned the deed to the lot and later built a home on it.

The most unusual story about that same house was that I made forty-five separate insurance sales to people who helped

I "bought" the lot for the first home I built by selling other houses the owner had not been able to sell.

build the house. The most remarkable sale occurred on my way home one day. When I stopped by to see how the new house was progressing, a man was soldering a gutter on the house. Just for fun I climbed up on the other side of the house and came down the roof toward him, opened my briefcase, and started talking to him. He burst out laughing and said, "You are either crazy or the most resourceful insurance salesman I have ever met in my life. I am going to buy from you just because of your ingenuity." I sold him a policy, and he became one of my good friends and an excellent center of influence. Every time he would introduce me to somebody, he would tell the story about my presentation to him on the roof. This rooftop story "broke the ice" and made it easy for me to get an appointment and then to make a sale.

Meeting needs and making friends have been the most gratifying aspects of my sales career. One special recognition I received reflects the friendships I developed as well as the appreciation these friends felt for me. This recognition occurred in Columbus, Georgia, twenty years after I moved from that city. The countless policyholders I had sold insurance to staged a "Paul J. Meyer Appreciation Day."

The half-a-cow story, *Souris* (the ever-selling yacht), trading an insurance policy for a hotel, and the others I have told here are just a few experiences to show you how much fun I have had. I just wish others in sales would have as much fun as I have had and would make as many friends as I have made. I loved "bartering for business," but I would not trade anything for the fun I have had and the lifelong friends I have made!

23

I WAS FIRED FROM EVERY JOB I EVER HAD

THE FIRST JOB **I ever had was picking prunes** when I was six years old. My dad drove to the end of Shelley Avenue at White Oaks Road and left me there to work in the orchards with a group of migrant workers. The foreman protested to my dad that I was too young to work. My dad responded, "Well, we want him to *learn* to work."

He gave me the job. In one day I picked only one box of prunes, and the man gave me a nickel. The man told my dad that I played too much and did not work like I was supposed to. *So he fired me*!

My second job was cutting apricots for our neighbors, the Farnhams. The procedure involved cutting the apricots (or "cots," as they were called), removing the pits, and then putting them on a large four-by-six tray. Next the trays of "cots" were put in the sun to dry. Because I did not keep my focus and pay attention, and I distracted others from working—*I was fired.*

The third job I was fired from really bothered me because Mr. Beal and I were good friends. I worked for Mr. Beal picking apricots. The workers at that time were paid fifty cents an hour. When I asked Mr. Beal how many boxes of apricots the workers picked on an average during the day, he said, "About one box per hour." I commented to him, "I would like to work in 'piece' work." This meant that I wanted to work for fifty cents a box. Mr. Beal agreed.

I found that if I sped up I could pick twice as many apricots as everybody else and, of course, make twice as much money. The mistake I made was sharing my strategy with one of the other younger migrant farm workers who shared it with another person. Finally some of the workers told Mr. Beal they wanted to be paid the same way I was paid—by the box—or they were going to quit. Mr. Beal talked to me and explained how much he liked me, but that he could not afford to let all twenty of the other workers go. *So he fired me.*

On another occasion I worked for Mr. Mirassou, founder of the Mirassou Wineries, hoeing around grapevines. Mr. Mirassou explained that the workers were being paid fifty cents an hour, and they worked between thirty-five and fifty grapevines per hour. Because it was more motivational to me, I asked him if I could work "piece" work and get one penny for each vine. I averaged eighty-three vines per hour, so I made eighty-three cents each hour. This time I did not tell anybody about my work agreement. But somehow the other workers found out. For all I knew, Mr. Mirassou might have told them I was doing 50 percent more work than they were doing. So Mr. Mirassou let me go for the same reason Mr. Beal did. That is, all the workers were going to quit *en masse*, which he could not afford. *So he fired me.*

As an adult, the first sales job I had was with Independent Life & Accident Insurance Company in Columbus, Georgia, where I quickly became the leading producer in the company. At the end of a year I wanted a promotion or some acknowledgment other than "Thank you, you did great." I wanted to be a manager, but I was told I was too young—the company did not have any managers as young as I was.

Jealousy was rampant in the office of approximately forty people. I was considered an outsider because most of the people had grown up in that town, and I had not. I got into a heated discussion with the manager, and he told me it was time I "moved on." In protest, I went to the company headquarters in Jacksonville to see the president, Mr. Snead, who told me he had to support the manager's decision. Mr. Snead gave me some advice that proved far more valuable than a job with his company, "Selfishly, I would like to find some other place for you, but frankly, we just have weekly premium debit insurance in this company. You could probably do better selling ordinary insurance." *So I was fired, but ever so diplomatically!*

The next company I worked with was called Acme Insurance, which has since merged with another company ... which merged with another company ... which merged with yet another company. I also led Acme Insurance from the beginning, and the same thing happened. I was ambitious and expressed my desire for advancement. Again, I was told I was too young for advancement. I did not quit, *but I was soon fired by the agency head.* The only explanation I could figure out was that I threatened his job, which was probably true because I wanted more responsibility and authority.

After that I went to work for the world's largest exclusive ordinary insurance company, Franklin Life Insurance Company, which has five thousand salespeople. The entire time I was with the company I also led it. For example, I sold 140 policies in the first sixty days for over one million dollars face amount of life insurance. The fellow who had the rights to the South Florida territory did not want to give up part of his territory to let me have an equal agency so he simply fired me. Again, I appealed to the president, Mr. Charles Becker, but he said he had to go with management's decision. He was willing to give me an opportunity in some other part of the United States, but at that time I did not want to move from South Florida. So I was "gone again."

Next I went to work with a new, young life insurance company called National Union—an Alabama company that was relatively new in Florida. I felt I had a better opportunity in this situation because I had the contract to produce all of their insurance in three states—Georgia, Alabama, and Florida. In addition to my own selling, I aggressively built a life insurance agency, one of the largest and most successful in the country. In fact, that agency wrote more life insurance than the company had the reserves to cover. This put the company in jeopardy with the insurance commissioner of the state of Florida. As a result, our entire agency force had to stop producing insurance. I would not exactly say we were fired, but *we were all forced to stop working*. To me, it was *the same thing as being fired*.

One unusual job I was fired from involved selling franchises for countertop dispensers for grape juice, orange juice, and hot chocolate. I had just started the job. I went with this company to learn about franchising and that type of marketing because I knew very little about it. I thought the best way to learn would be to immerse myself as an apprentice in this industry because in the back of my mind the idea of starting SMI was beginning to form. I wanted to know every kind of available marketing so I would select the right way to market the programs and ideas I intended to produce sometime in the future. Mr. Brunchen, who owned the H. A. Brunchen Company, fired me. But I could hardly blame him. Listen to my story.

After I had been with the company for about a month, I learned more about its internal workings. In typical Paul Meyer investigative style, I was asking question after question of every employee, department by department, and taking copious notes. After about thirty days and evaluating my research, it was my opinion the company was not going to be able to deliver what the management told me to tell prospective franchisees. I wondered what to do, but then I remembered what I was taught as a young person. "Do the right thing because it's the right thing to do." So I asked Mr. Brunchen if we could have a meeting, and I shared with him my concerns. He said I was young, I did not understand, I was incorrect, and I should just do my job of selling the franchises.

That did not set well with me because I believed I had become as successful as I had to date by relying on my instincts. I soon found out I was dead right. So what did I do about it? Amazingly, and brazenly, I called the people to whom I had already sold the franchises. I told them to cancel their checks or to take advantage of the buy-back clause in the contract because I had discovered something about the company that was not totally correct. I told them I did not have confidence that what I had told them when they bought their franchise would actually work out. Obviously when this got back to Mr. Brunchen, he not only censured me in a way I would rather not describe to you, *but he also fired me on the spot.* I thank God for what I learned from this short tenure, but I am most thankful that my character and integrity remained intact 100 percent.

My first job in Texas was with a young company called Word Records—later changed to Word, Inc. Again, I was the leading cash producer in that company, bringing in a considerable amount of money. I was instrumental at increasing sales 1,500 percent in two years. After a successful annual convention, I was called to a board meeting where the board members told me they wanted to reduce my compensation because I was making "too much" money—more than the key players. I would not accept their reducing my compensation. *So they fired me.*

With the prior permission of the Word board, I had just started Success Motivation Institute on the side. My objective in joining Word Records in the first place was to learn about the record industry. I wanted to condense self-improvement books and put the condensations on twelve-inch LPs. I also wanted to write and produce courses. So Word, Inc., actually did me a favor. The board just fired me a year ahead of when I had planned to leave anyway.

As I have grown older, I am even more convinced that these firings were blessings in disguise because they stimulated my entrepreneurial spirit and nurtured a sense of independence. In retrospect, I can clearly see how my first entrepreneurial venture foreshadowed things to come. On this occasion I took some bold initiative. I decided that to keep from getting fired, I would make a deal with a farmer. Instead of working directly as a fruit picker I would ask a farmer to sign a contract with me to pick all the fruit and then let me hire the kids to work for me. My first attempt with this was with Mr. Stein, who owned twenty acres of prune orchards. He agreed to pay me to pick prunes at twenty-five cents a box. I hired the other kids in school and had them sign a contract that I would pay them twenty cents a box. I made five cents override, but out of my override I had to pay for the shakers to shake the trees. The kids did well because this arrangement provided employment for the entire summer. I did well because I made the override. In addition, I challenged myself every day to pick more than the other kids. I always met that challenge. I also met the terms of my contract. I was not fired from that job because *I was my own boss.*

I must admit I have no regrets because I learned a great deal from each of these rungs up the ladder of success. For one thing, I also found out in the process of my fifty-some-odd years of business experience that I am obviously by nature an entrepreneur. I also learned to make sure not to treat people the same way I had been treated. The principles I learned were these:

1. Be sure as owner or manager to structure all compensations fairly.
2. Treat people the way you would like to be treated.
3. Pay people commensurate with their capacity and capability to produce as opposed to a "set amount" for a "set job."
4. Pick the right person for the right job at the right time. No two of us are alike. We are all different. We always have been, and we always will be.

Many of my friends, family, and associates have joked with me over the years about my fetish for wanting to own control of all the Meyer Family Enterprise companies. It is true that either my family or I own 100 percent of at least 90 percent of the forty-plus companies we have an interest in. But I fear that if I did not own control of each company, somebody… somewhere… some way… somehow… *would fire me.*

I have to admit that to own the company is the only way I have been able to hold a job for the last thirty-five years!

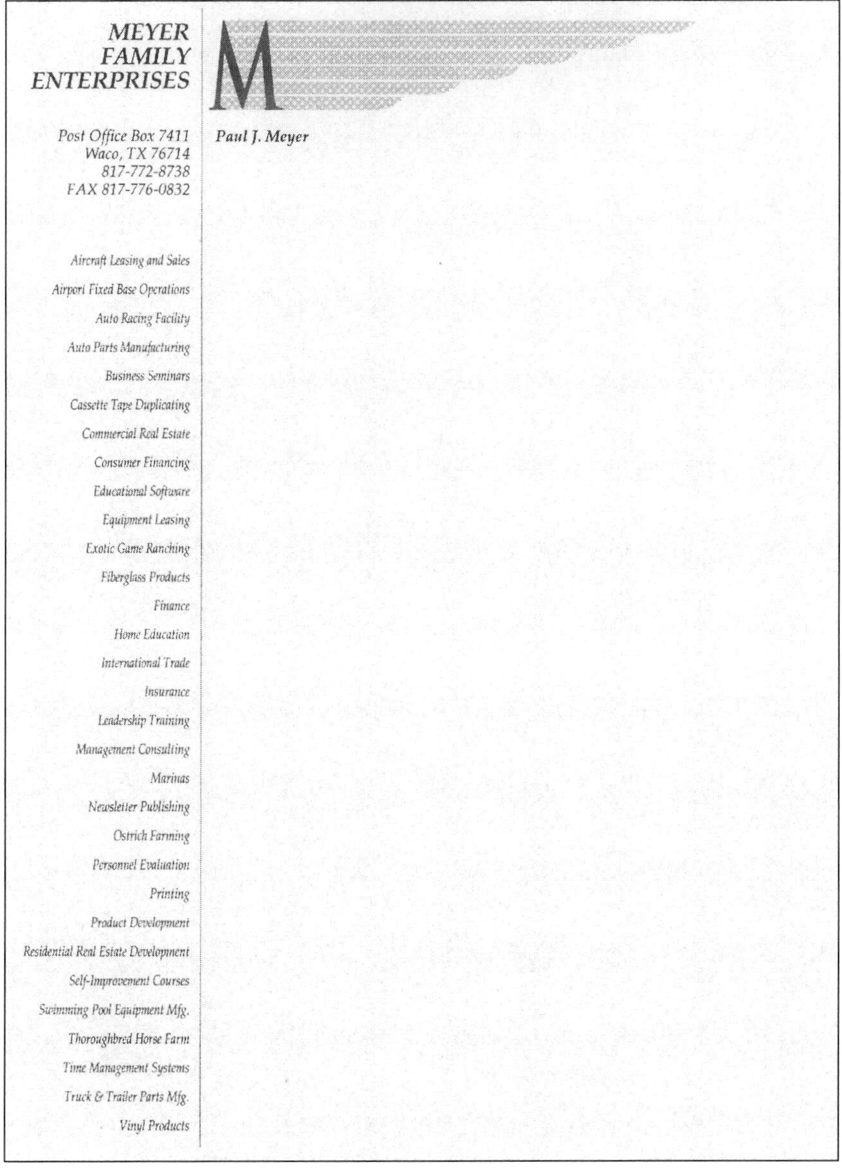

MEYER
FAMILY
ENTERPRISES

Post Office Box 7411
Waco, TX 76714
817-772-8738
FAX 817-776-0832

Paul J. Meyer

Aircraft Leasing and Sales
Airport Fixed Base Operations
Auto Racing Facility
Auto Parts Manufacturing
Business Seminars
Cassette Tape Duplicating
Commercial Real Estate
Consumer Financing
Educational Software
Equipment Leasing
Exotic Game Ranching
Fiberglass Products
Finance
Home Education
International Trade
Insurance
Leadership Training
Management Consulting
Marinas
Newsletter Publishing
Ostrich Farming
Personnel Evaluation
Printing
Product Development
Residential Real Estate Development
Self-Improvement Courses
Swimming Pool Equipment Mfg.
Thoroughbred Horse Farm
Time Management Systems
Truck & Trailer Parts Mfg.
Vinyl Products

Entrepreneurship is obviously my strength, not working for someone else. My family and I own more than forty companies—the general areas are listed on my business stationery.

24

MR. ENTHUSIASM—MY FRIEND BILL

MOST OF US, I imagine, would describe an enthusiastic person as someone who is alert, alive, effervescent, happy, smiling, eager, confident, possessing a good self-image, a lover of life—all of the above and much, much more. That sums up Mr. Enthusiasm, my friend Bill.

I first met Bill Armor more than forty-four years ago when we were about twenty-four years of age. Even at that early age, Bill had it all: personality plus, backed with integrity, character, and honesty that could be matched by only a few individuals I have met in my lifetime. One of the most amazing aspects of our relationship is that I do not have a closer friend who knows the core of my being any better than Bill—or vice versa. Yet we have lived most of the last forty years over a thousand miles from each other in different parts of the country. But I still count Bill among my top five friends of a lifetime.

I know this for certain: If the chips were down and I had exhausted all available sources of help to do something I wanted to do, or if I were in need and I had used up all of my resources, all I would have to do is give Bill a call. He would drop what he was doing and be there for me. How many people do you know in a lifetime you can say that about? For me—I suppose for all of us—the number is very small.

Bill has been a friend, a business associate, a partner, a confidant, and a compadre. He has been there in good times and bad times, high times and low times. His spirit is amazingly buoyant and high all the time. He can always be counted on to be steadfast. I know the sky will get dark at night, and it will be light again in the morning—and I know I can depend on Bill.

> Bill's genuine, heartfelt enthusiasm created confidence that cries to the world, "I've got what it takes!"

When did we start calling Bill "Mr. Enthusiasm"? I do not remember exactly, but I think it began on a golf course and proceeded to the office of Dr. Roger Stockton, a dentist in Florida. Guys joke a lot on a golf course and they challenge one another, sometimes becoming silly, absurd, and even borderline ridiculous. My forty-four year memory of this situation recalls how it evolved into the borderline ridiculous because Bill bragged that he could get in to see *anybody—anywhere, anytime, anyplace*—while still wearing his golf shoes and carrying his golf clubs.

His infectious enthusiasm also captured our interest—we immediately accepted Bill's challenge. "We'll bet you! Let's see you do it."

In less than forty-five minutes we arrived at Dr. Stockton's dental office. With his flashing smile and effervescent enthusiasm, Bill charged in and told the nurse, "I need to see the doctor instantly. It's a matter of life or death." (We were selling *life* insurance, so I suppose that was a somewhat accurate statement.) The startled nurse pointed toward the doctor's office. As usual, Bill's zeal was contagious and persuasive. His enthusiasm swayed the nurse into instant harmony with his goal—getting in to see the doctor!

Dr. Stockton was working on a patient when Bill opened the door and told the patient, "You will have to wait a few minutes because I must see the doctor immediately!" In a matter of minutes Bill's good humor and charm totally captivated and captured Dr. Stockton's attention. Bill easily sold him a life insurance policy. His enthusiasm persuaded without pressure. It sparked an excitement that shouted an irresistible invitation: "Wake up and *live*!" His enthusiasm blasted every obstacle from his path. (In this case, the patient was the obstacle. But there is no doubt in my mind that patient benefited as much from Bill's contagious enthusiasm as from the doctor's treatment.)

The best part of that story is that it was typical of all Bill's sales. His enthusiasm drew that doctor to him and electrified him with positive thinking—and created an instant bond. Roger Stockton became one of Bill's half-dozen or so best friends for the next forty-some-odd years. They have enjoyed fishing trips together, camping trips, hunting trips, golf trips—you name it—and it all started as a bet on a golf course in Fort Lauderdale, Florida.

If the price and the deal are right, many people compromise their principles to make the deal. Not Bill Armor! I remember when an insurance company I was associated with ran into difficulty—their ox was in the ditch. Everybody *scattered like rats on a sinking ship*. Not Bill—he was uncompromising and unrelenting. His enthusiasm was sincere and profound. For more than a year we helped several hundred agents find new jobs, helped collect the company's insurance premiums, and helped straighten out a mess created by the company's mismanagement. His enthusiasm paved the way for new ideas and novel solutions. His effervescent personality energized us with positive expectancy throughout the entire ordeal. In addition, it was an educational experience for both of us, and it solidified and secured our friendship in a way that no other experience could ever have done. I can never repay Bill for helping me at the lowest point of my life. But Bill does not *expect* to be repaid—and he does not *want* to be repaid.

As young men, Bill and I talked about what we would like to do with our lives. Bill said that someday he would like to be president of a life insurance company. I told him about my desires to be in the self-improvement business. We helped and encouraged each other. Bill took courses in life insurance company management in Dallas. We made contacts, networked, and within thirty-six months Bill became president of a life insurance company and moved to Casper, Wyoming. I moved to Texas and started Success Motivation Institute, Inc.

One of the many illustrious Bill Armor stories involves a prospect for a yacht we wanted to sell. We were driving through an intersection in Bill's limousinelike Cadillac. I was in the backseat, and our prospect was sitting next to me. A young man traveling too fast hit us broadside and spun our car around. Our prospective customer's door flew open and he sailed out of the car. The first thing Bill said was, "There goes our prospect."

As soon as we knew our prospect was not hurt, we became hysterical with laughter. He looked like ten dogs had chewed on him for about two days. His shoes were all scuffed, his hands and knees were skinned up, and his suit was torn and tattered. Bill smiled, laughed, and *cheered the guy up*—even had him laughing with us. That is what made the whole thing unbelievable. But

Bill always had that magic about him. I think in any person's darkest hour, or any group's low point, or any negative situation, Bill could come on the scene and in just a matter of minutes have everyone laughing and smiling and happy. That is the special gift of Mr. Enthusiasm, my friend Bill.

Another time Bill and I were assisting a friend trying to sell a hot chocolate machine to a man in South Carolina. The Helmco-Lacy chocolate dispenser was mounted on a temporary stand with a motor similar to a sewing machine motor below it. The blender could whip the chocolate to make it taste like the kind grandma makes. To help our friend, we were talking to Mr. Black about making an investment in a new company that wanted to market these machines. Bill proceeded to demonstrate the machine. When he pulled down on the handle, the machine broke and spilled and splattered the chocolate everywhere. Then Bill started laughing; then I began laughing, and soon Mr. Black was laughing. It was one of the funniest Marx Brothers' type scenes I have ever seen!

The *funniest* experience was related to me by one of Bill's clients in about 1954. I received a phone call from a man who owned a hardware store in Fort Lauderdale. He said he wanted to speak to the agency head in the home office. I said, "I'm that person." He then went to great lengths to assure me that he was not dissatisfied, nor was he complaining. He said a young man had sold him an insurance contract he wanted very much to buy. He asked, "I wonder if you could explain to me in more detail what I bought?"

Right away I guessed who had sold him: Mr. Enthusiasm, my friend Bill! I asked, "Was he about five feet, eight inches, with blondish hair, a smile from ear to ear, and bouncing like a kangaroo?" The man burst into laughter and said, "Yeah, that's him." I said, "Well, I can answer your question. But before I do,

I'd like to ask you one. Why would you give your money to someone to buy something you didn't fully understand?" He replied, "Oh, Mr. Meyer, you didn't see him come in the door, and you didn't see him walk down the aisle between our cases, and you didn't hear his presentation. He's the most excitable, enthusiastic, electrifying, and charming young man who has ever been in here. I just enjoyed spending time with him. He brightened my whole day. I hope he comes back and comes back often!"

The conclusion of the story is that Bill sold this grateful man a half dozen more times and, of course, became his friend. This extraordinary gentleman cherished his friendship with my friend Bill.

On another occasion Bill and I were in the home of a gentleman who said he was too busy to talk to us. He explained that he had to leave, but his wife would probably be interested in talking to us. After Bill made his presentation, she said, "Well, I want to do some business with you." She went over to a drawer in her kitchen, opened it, and took out more than $50,000 worth of securities: AT&T, Texaco, and other miscellaneous stock certificates—over twenty different companies with small pieces of stock. She said, "Here, I'll buy whatever these are worth. Check with the broker, and I'll take one of the high-premium life insurance contracts." I know who I can sell and who I cannot sell, and I would not have been able to sell that woman—not now or not in a million years! But Bill sold her—easily and in no time at all.

Bill was with me the time we traded the life insurance policy for a hotel. He was with me when we sold the yacht over and over again. He was with me as we made hundreds of life insurance sales. Bill's enthusiasm enabled him to bring more *vim*, *vigor*, *vitality*, and *vibrance* to any meeting, anytime, anywhere, than anyone else I have ever known. Time spent with Bill is always the best of the best.

I regret I do not live closer to Bill and have not been able to spend more time with him in the last forty-five years. I have frequently used Bill as an illustration in speeches, in articles, and in talking with salespeople. Bill is the best example I have ever known in my lifetime of the benefits you can gain and enjoy from being enthusiastic about life and living.

Bill's enthusiasm permeates every facet of his life. His optimism radiates a message to all those around him that he is happy, at peace with himself, confident, and prosperous in all of his endeavors—including his friendships. I have been yachting, golfing, hunting, dry fly-fishing, and just plain relaxing and having a good time with him. Nearly everyone Bill meets becomes his friend because, on a social basis, no one can have more fun than being with Bill.

Enthusiasm is the most contagious emotion, the most powerful communication, the most effective motivator. No wonder everyone who knows my friend Bill calls him "Mr. Enthusiasm"!

For the past twenty-five years or so, Bill and his wife Joyce have lived six months in Casper, Wyoming, and six months in Stuart, Florida. Bill fishes one day and plays golf the next, is always working on charity projects in his community, and spends time with his children and grandchildren.

Bill has two sons and a daughter. I know one of the sons, Dale, very well, and he is like a son to me. Bill's genes and passion for living have obviously been passed on to Dale. Most of all, Dale is following in his dad's footsteps in the most important area: his values—his honesty, his character, his integrity.

Enthusiasm has long been celebrated by poets, philosophers, and others. Ralph Waldo Emerson said, "Nothing great was ever achieved without enthusiasm." Bill Armor's life validates this truth. His heartfelt enthusiasm has encouraged, inspired, and empowered countless individuals. I count myself fortunate to be one of them. And so I say "Thanks!" to my friend Bill—Mr. Enthusiasm!

25

MY FIRST . . .

MY CHILDREN, grandchildren, and friends frequently ask questions like, "Do you still remember your first day of school?" or "Do you remember the first time you saw the ocean, or the first time you saw a movie?" I have been fortunate that my life has been enriched with many meaningful memories—memories that have played a part in shaping my attitudes and the kind of person I am. Here are just a few of them.

The first picnic I remember was at Alamarock Park. We had German potato salad, some roast beef sandwiches, and fruit. We had fruit juice to drink. At this picnic was also my first time ever to see a giant swimming pool with a big slide. I can remember the entire trip as though it were just last summer—packing for the picnic and going in the car with my mother, dad, brother, and sister. I can also remember the joy I felt just being with my family. Family has always been important to me—and always will be!

My first time to see the ocean was in Santa Cruz, California, when I was about four years old. We had gone there for a picnic. I have loved the ocean ever since. Jane and I have spent at least five years of our life together on the seashore.

My first cross-country automobile trip was from California to Michigan when I was five years old. My dad drove a 1932 Chevrolet Tudor Sedan. Out of my nostalgia, I bought a 1932 Chevrolet Sedan in Kalamazoo, Michigan, a few years ago.

My first time to ride a horse was at my grandmother and grandfather's home in Kalamazoo, Michigan. It was a plow horse. But to me it could have been Secretariat because I was five years old, the sun was shining, and I was ecstatic over my first horse ride. I remember afterward lying in the hay and playing with my brother and sister. It was a warm day. It was wonderful! (I am the happy one in the middle.)

My first day of school was in September 1934. I was six years old. About twelve pupils were in the first grade. Our teacher was Mrs. McCormack. What I remember most about that first day of school is that I wet my pants because I was too afraid to tell the teacher I had to go to the bathroom.

My first day to work and earn money was at age six picking prunes. I earned a nickel that day. It is amazing how proud a person can feel about an accomplishment like that at such a young age.

The first Christmas I remember was on Shelley Avenue in Campbell, California. I was six years old. My dad had made my brother a wagon, and I got a pencil box and some walnuts and oranges for Christmas. I do not think I ever had a better Christmas as a child.

The first birthday party I remember was when I was seven. All the students in my class came to my house. Back then no one had any money; so everyone brought whatever their family had raised or could make:

- A hand-carved knife from one of the boys, which I still had over twenty years later and used as a letter opener
- Some strawberries from Buddy Takata that his family raised
- Some artichokes from Arthur Grecko that his family raised
- Some shelled walnuts from one of the other boys
- Some vegetables from another
- Handmade birthday cards from some of the girls

My mother made my birthday cake and some punch. We all had a great time!

My first encounter with death was the death of my grandmother when I was eight years old. My first encounter with the death of a good friend was when my closest friend,

Billy, burned to death in a sleeping bag on a Scout trip. I was twelve years old.

My first cat was black and white. It was just a stray—but I loved that little cat. And I have loved cats ever since. Now I have a backyard cat, white and brown, named "Princess," and a front-yard cat, an orange one, named "Morris."

The first pants I remember wearing were knickers. I wore these to school and to church. The first pair of long pants I remember wearing was when I was nine years old. I could not wait—it always bothered me that I was the only one who wore knickers from the day I started school at age six until I was nine. All the other boys wore long pants starting at age six. I felt like I had really grown up on that day.

The first movie I remember was *Stagecoach*. I remember it well! John Wayne was the leading man, and this movie was one of the many in which he portrayed the American cowboy hero—courageous but kind and hardworking, with a compelling sense of justice.

The first book I remember reading was *Black Beauty*, the life story of a beloved and beautiful black stallion, beginning with his early carefree days. His destiny was to be sold to many masters, some cruel, some ignorant of how to treat a horse, and some who loved him but were too poor to keep him. As Black Beauty grew up, he never forgot the rules his mother taught him, regardless of his situation. The heartwarming conclusion of *Black Beauty* is a classic reminder that doing right always pays off in the long run. I loved this book and read it several times.

My first time to ride a roller coaster was in Santa Cruz, California, when I was about twelve years old. I remember very clearly that of the eight or ten of us on the ride, two became very ill with an upset stomach. As for me? I never did anything else at the entertainment park at the Wharf that was more exciting.

My first bike came from the junkyard. My dad helped me take it apart, straighten the frame, and put it back together. That was when I fell in love with working on bikes. I made a good bit of money from ages thirteen through sixteen, buying, repairing, and selling bikes.

My first sales job as a teenager was selling magazines. I loved it! I had a chance to meet a lot of people. The older ladies always gave me cookies and treated me kindly. I was the leading producer in the nation for *Ladies' Home Journal*, *Liberty Magazine*, and the *Saturday Evening Post*. This was in 1939, 1940, and 1941.

The first sport I played was basketball. I took to it like a duck to water. I practiced shooting baskets by the hour on a handmade hoop in our backyard. I excelled in basketball.

My first new coat was bought with my own money when I was fourteen. Up until then I had worn hand-me-downs from an older brother and three older cousins: plenty to wear—really nice—but not brand new.

My first date was with a girl named Donna Baker. I must have been fourteen or fifteen. We went to what they called the "sock hop" after school. I took her a bouquet of sweet peas. I was scared to death. I danced with her only one dance.

My first time as a patient in a hospital was at age sixteen when I had my appendix removed. I remember riding 105 miles per hour in the doctor's red Cadillac convertible. Several miles from the hospital my appendix ruptured. I was in surgery two and a half hours. The next twelve months I gained fifty pounds and grew nine inches in height.

The first car I owned myself was a 1931 Model-A Coupe with a rumble seat. The first car I remember being allowed to use was my brother's 1936 Ford Cabriolet. Although Carl owned the car, he told me I could call it half mine if I took care of it. As a result of that car and the opportunity my brother gave me with it, I fell in love with 1936 Fords and have since started a collection of them. I now have eighteen different 1936 Ford vehicles.

My first ride on a train was a troop train going from Sacramento, California, to Fort Jackson, South Carolina, in 1946. It was hot, crowded, and slow. But I was proud to be serving my country.

My first airplane ride came after I had joined the army and became part of the United States Paratroopers. Actually, I took off in an airplane eighteen times and jumped out before I ever landed while still in a plane. I also remember the first time I landed; the plane slowed down and turned on a base leg before turning on final approach. I thought it was going so slow that it was going to crash, and I wished I had my parachute so I could jump out rather than have to land.

My first sexual experience was on my wedding night.

My first job after serving in the U.S. Paratroopers was selling life insurance. My first sale was to an elderly lady on Short Lawyers Lane in Columbus, Georgia. She introduced me to everybody on her street. That helped me to lead that agency in that town my first day in the business, which started a trend: I was never second during my entire insurance-selling career.

My first business venture as an adult was investing in a dump truck that had painted on the side of it "Paul J. Meyer—Topsoil, Sand, and Gravel" and my phone number. I had three dump trucks. One of my drivers took my gas and destroyed a truck. Another one kept some of the funds. This first business ended up being a loss.

My first time to pilot an airplane occurred in my early twenties. I flew a Piper Cub at Brown Field in South Miami. I have been flying ever since. Since reaching the age of sixty-five, I have made over two thousand landings in my yellow Piper Cub.

My first time to scuba dive was in 1971. My son Larry and I were taught by a man named Orley. Our first dive was in Lake Travis near Austin, Texas. Since then I have enjoyed diving in a dozen other places around the world, including the Great Barrier Reef, Mexico, Hawaii, some of the Caribbean islands, and of course, the Cayman Islands. The best diving by far has been in the Cayman Islands.

My first time to snow ski was at Lake Tahoe in 1971. The people we were with said I needed an instructor. I said I did not need any lessons. Jane said she thought we should have at least *some*. I said, "I don't need any instructions. Just give me the skis. It's a matter of putting the skis on and pointing them downhill." And that is exactly what I did. I put them on, pointed them downhill, and took off. I could not stop and wiped out an entire lift-line of approximately forty people. I do not know exactly what they were saying, but I think it was profanity in about four different languages! When I picked myself up, I admitted to Jane, "I am now ready for an instructor to show me how to do this correctly."

My first time to watch the birth of a baby was October 8, 1974, in Waco, Texas, when our daughter Leslie Jane Meyer was born. I was scared! Back then they would not allow fathers into the delivery room to watch their babies born. But I talked my way into the delivery room. As I was holding my wife's hand and looking into her face, the doctor said to me, "You wanted to see this so bad. I just want to tell you—you are at the wrong end!" Somewhat embarrassed, I changed positions. Seeing Leslie born was an incredible experience!

The first time I went on a cruise ship was in 1980, and it was out of Miami. Jane tells me that all our friends bet that I was too active and could not stand a cruise ship. Sure enough, after only one night, we reached the Cayman Islands, and I asked the captain whether we were going someplace prettier. When he said "No," I said, "Adios! I am getting off here." He said, "You can't get a refund." I told him, "Keep the change. It was worth it just to find this place!"

My first time to drive a car in a race was the first two weeks of June 1996. The qualifications required driving a pre-1940 car. I drove a 1936 Ford Sedan Delivery with Gene Franklin as navigator. We drove forty-five hundred miles from Tacoma, Washington, to Toronto, Ontario, on the back roads of the U.S. and Canada. We stopped in forty-seven towns and stayed in fifteen different hotels. Meeting many wonderful people was the highlight of this exciting experience.

My first time to use a personal computer has yet to happen! There are thousands of PCs in the companies I own and operate. I marvel at what can be done with computers, but I prefer to hire computer experts while I do the thinking, pursue entrepreneurial opportunities, and engage in other activities that provide jobs for the computer experts and others.

The first time I found out my father changed his name to "Meyer" when he immigrated to the United States from Germany was in the fall of 1995. But that is another subject for another story to be told at another time…

26

LOVING THE DIFFERENCE

INTERNATIONAL INVOLVEMENT early in my business life gave me a great appreciation for diversity in the marketplace long before the experts started discussing it. I have good business friends all over the world. I have been professionally and personally enriched by interactions with people whose skin color is different from mine, who speak a different language, who eat different foods, and who maintain entirely different lifestyles.

As Jane and I enjoy each additional year of our marriage, I find myself applying what I have observed in business to what I see in marriage relationships—especially my own but also in the relationships and marriages of our adult children and others. When I consider the diversity—the differences—in our marriage, I am stunned at the sharp contrasts:

I am male.	*She is female.*
I am from California.	*She is from Texas.*

I roll my toothpaste tube up from the bottom.	*She squeezes hers in the middle.*
I like muffins.	*She prefers bagels.*
I like marinara sauce on my pasta.	*She likes meat sauce.*
I like Italian salad dressing.	*She likes creamy ranch.*
I like smooth peanut butter.	*She likes crunchy.*
I like orange juice on my cereal.	*She prefers milk.*
I like rice cereal.	*She likes oats.*
I like to sit in the shade.	*She likes to sit in the sun.*
I like western music.	*She likes easy listening.*
I like antique cars.	*She likes new cars.*
I like basketball.	*She likes football.*
I like warm rooms.	*She likes cold rooms.*
I like bicycle exercise.	*She likes the treadmill and walking for exercise.*
I like adventure films.	*She likes tearjerkers.*
I like brass instruments.	*She likes strings.*
I like toilet paper coming off the top of the roll.	*She likes it coming off the bottom.*
I like cats.	*She likes dogs.*
I read business publications.	*She reads novels.*
I like audiocassettes.	*She likes videos.*
I like the desert.	*She likes the mountains.*
I like the country.	*She likes New York City.*
I like the color red.	*She likes red too!*

Is our both liking the color red the basis for a strong marriage? I hardly think so! We enjoy other likenesses as well. We both like the beach, movies, tennis, and golf. My search for likenesses soon switched to more serious issues. We both love our children. We both respect the personhood, individuality, and rights of each other and all people. The more I think about marriage, the more intriguing I find it; successful marriages are an almost unexplainable phenomenon. I have seen incredibly happy marriages with partners as different as day and night. In contrast, I have seen happy marriages of two people who are almost clones of each other, who seem to think and act as if one brain were in control; one's thoughts and actions are a mirror image of the other's.

Which is better? Differences and diversity? Or likenesses and similarity? The key to successful, satisfying marriages, I have concluded, is somewhat similar to success in business. Success cannot be explained by simplistic rules, nor can success be analyzed accurately with sweeping generalizations. Certain basic rules of thumb, however, characterize any successful interaction—in marriage or in business. Respecting one another and not trying to impose one's own opinions of what is right on the other are imperative. Some adaptation and accommodation is essential, of course, for people to coexist or transact business. But change is never forced, coerced, or insisted upon in a satisfying, long-lasting relationship. When one insists that changes be made, resentment often festers and destroys trust and unconditional acceptance—both essentials for a dynamic, fulfilling relationship in either marriage or business. Constructive change grows out of respect and concern for the other person—not from a judgmental or self-righteous compulsion to control the other person's thinking or behavior.

I enjoy interacting with people all over the world and doing business with them. I would not insult any of these individuals by insisting or even insinuating that they should think just as I think, dress just as I dress, eat the same food I eat, talk just as I talk. So why in the world would I be so presumptuous as to insult my marriage partner by insisting or even suggesting that she change how she thinks and how she behaves simply to please my preferences? If Jane and I were just alike, our lives would be as boring as going to a banquet table filled with all the dishes of food just alike. The most festive culinary delight, the most inviting, appealing banquet, offers a vast array of delicious dishes. Similarly, two individuals bring to marriage different experiences and expectations from their entire lifetime and from each day's activities to create an intriguing feast. Both have something distinctive, unique, and interesting to bring to the party!

I remember clearly one day about twenty years ago coming into our family room after a great day of business negotiating and wheeling and dealing. I asked Jane, "How's everything going?" She answered, "I've had a rough day." I asked, "What's it about?" She explained quickly that it had something to do with the house. My instantaneous response was, "No big deal. I'll just call the guy who has done that kind of work for us before."

Then Jane mentioned something else bothering her, and I answered, "Don't worry about it, I'll take care of it." After about five or six of this kind of exchanges, she stopped me and said, "You are discounting me." I was stunned; I said, "Oops, translate that for me. I don't understand what you mean." She explained, "I don't want you to fix what is broken, and I don't want you to call the repairmen. I just want you to listen to how I feel about what has happened to me today. I want to share my feelings with you." Jane continued, "If you will turn off your business motor and just sit down and be Paul instead of Mr. Meyer at the office, I have something I want to share with you. I want you to listen to me because you love me and want to understand me. You did ask me how my day was, didn't you? I am trying to tell you how my day was. I want you to listen to what I have to say about my day, and I want you to pay attention to my feelings, not tell me how you'll fix everything. Just listen!"

Respecting each other's right to feel, think, and act in our own unique way has strengthened the love Jane and I have for one another.

"Okay," I answered—and I listened, *really* listened. When she looked at me in anticipation of a response, I said, "I want to thank you for telling me that you feel I discount you. I was not aware that I was doing that to you. I can't tell you how much I appreciate your sharing with me and communicating your feelings with me. I love you too much to discount you or minimize your feelings. I want you to know I value you as a person, and I am concerned about how you feel. I want to understand how you see things, and I want to know how you feel about them." That day twenty years ago was a watershed, a milestone; that open, honest, insightful communication was a turning point in our relationship because it made us both realize our very different ways of seeing things and our very different ways of responding to them.

A film shown in a psychology course I took at Purdue University illustrates a principle at work in that interaction with

Jane twenty years ago. The film, called *The Eye of the Beholder*, depicted a car wreck and what appeared to be a murder. Six people who saw the wreck were asked what they saw. Each one in turn described the wreck. Astonishingly, they all told dramatically different stories! This professional, twenty-minute film made an indelible impression on my mind; we are all different, we all see things from different perspectives, we all use different parts of our brain to interpret what we see and how we feel. The principle demonstrated so vividly in this film operates time and time again in my own life. So when Jane and I—or any family member, friend, or business associate—are communicating, I try to be perceptive, insightful, tuned in. I truly try to see things as they see them. I try to truly *listen* and understand what people are saying between the lines. I also respect the right of other people to their own opinions and their own feelings.

I envy people who have a thirty-minute or so ride home from work every day because this gives them time to switch from their business frame of mind to a mindset more conducive to a satisfying marriage. In the thirty-minute or so ride they can listen to their favorite music, sort through their thoughts, and regain the perspective that silence and solitude often provide. In short, they can disengage themselves from the business world and start concentrating on their marriage partner, family, and home. They can shift into a gear more appropriate for their particular family life. Because Jane and I have always lived in a smaller city, I am home within ten minutes or so. I have to make a conscious decision to shift gears quickly. My business success hinges on a take-charge, goal-oriented, bottom-line attitude and approach. Being a loving husband, father, and grandfather requires a different set of attitudes and behaviors. This *difference* can make a decisive *difference* in the success and satisfaction I achieve in business and in marriage.

"Variety is the spice of life" is a saying that I believe is at least mostly true—especially if the variety is mixed with a spirit of acceptance, respect, and cooperation. Over two thousand years ago, Plato supported the notion that opposites attract and that a husband and wife must be complementary and fit each other like the pieces of a jigsaw puzzle. People with very different viewpoints and personality traits are often drawn to each other because of the excitement and energy these dramatic opposites create. The initial attraction, however, can often soon wear away or turn into confusion and conflict. Opposites stay attracted to each other only when respect and acceptance of one's jagged edges are genuine and peaceful coalition is pursued. Otherwise when one partner expects the other to be in total agreement on everything, frustration and failure are almost inevitable; in that event, diversity results in adversity, contradictions, and confusion rather than creative cooperation and dynamic interaction.

The improvement of car tires, though an unlikely source of marital insight, provides a clear illustration of how differences and diversity can create a strong marriage if handled correctly. When cars were first invented, steel tires were used. These cast-iron circles withstood whatever punishment the rocky, unpaved, unpredictable roads meted out. But the passengers suffered rough, uncomfortable traveling. Later when rubber tires were developed, they provided a smoother ride but often wore away like melting butter. The brilliant idea finally struck someone of combining steel's toughness with rubber's ability to give a smoother ride—steel-belted tires!

Only when marriage partners respect each other's differences and avoid forcing change on one another can they weld their differences into a strong marriage. Only when they respect each other and the right of each to think and behave in different ways can they avoid turning the differences into adversities. They consciously work at using each unique difference as a basis for creating a steel-belted marriage strong enough to endure the bumps and to withstand the bruises of life, yet resilient enough to absorb the jolts and provide a pleasant journey throughout their marriage.

In my business interactions and in my marriage, I agree more and more enthusiastically with the French expression, "*Vive la diffèrence!*" I plan to continue accepting, appreciating, and enjoying diversity in my worldwide business, and I count on continuing to enjoy the dynamic enrichment of life created by my marriage with Jane—all the while *loving the difference!*

27

MONEY IS ONLY AN IDEA

"AM I GOING to have to do manual labor all of my life?" I remember asking my mother this heartfelt question shortly after my fifteenth birthday. The wisdom of her response profoundly influenced the direction of my life. She put her hands on my head—one hand on each side—and, looking me straight in the eyes, she said: "You have everything you need right here between your ears. In your head, you have everything you will ever need to take you anywhere you want to go, to have anything you want to have, and to be anything you want to be."

I believed her. At that moment I knew the world's abundance was mine—to earn and to possess. I could choose to remain a migrant fruit picker, or I could stake my claim on the world's resources and riches. The choice was mine, and everything depended on my attitude!

Over the years I have realized even more fully the powerful role attitude plays in determining success—including financial success. When people think of themselves as successful, they succeed. When they think of themselves as wealthy, they usually do what it takes to become wealthy. In contrast, people who *feel* inferior *act* inferior. People who consider themselves failures fail. People who think of themselves as poor remain poor. A poor self-image is an imposing, impenetrable barrier to achieving financial success.

I have chosen to think of myself as a success!

Attitude toward money itself also determines financial success. What I think about the nature of money is equally as forceful as what I think about myself and my potential for making money. My belief that *money is only an idea*, along with my positive self-image, is responsible for my success in earning money,

In *Building Financial Success* I explain some time-proven financial concepts that relate to earnings, savings, and investments. I also explain in depth the attitudes required for success in the accumulation of wealth—including the attitude that money is only an idea.

saving money, and investing money—and in accumulating assets.

Money itself has no intrinsic value. It is simply printed paper or minted metal worth no more than other paper or metal of comparable size and quality. The difference is made by money's exchange value. Authority and power have historically been vested in ownership. The person with the most tangible goods has always had an advantage because such goods may be traded for other assets—labor, raw materials, or additional goods. Since tangible wealth is cumbersome and in some cases absolutely immobile, money serves as a substitute—a token that represents valuable possessions.

The paper currency now in circulation consists merely of promissory notes guaranteed by the government. It is backed only by the faith people have in their government. The value of money lies in what others believe it is worth. Its value is based on belief and trust. In this context, money is only an idea. Understanding this concept has been vitally important to my desire and ability to attain financial success.

Most people respect money. A person of wealth once explained that even money has to *earn* our respect: "Anyone who doesn't spend time working is a disgrace, and money that is not working is even more disgraceful; it doesn't even have any aches and pains to excuse it." Sharing this pragmatic attitude toward money, few wealthy people have a lot of cash because it is invested. It is busy working for them, making more money. For people with wealth, money and its buying power hold no great sense of awe. It is money's investment power, the power to multiply itself, that commands the interest and attention of those who own it. As a result, most of the world's money is invested in assets other than cash. Most business transactions go on through credit. The credit card is rapidly replacing currency for the average consumer. "Plastic money" is neither tangible nor concrete; it is merely a concept, an idea.

Numerous other financial facts demonstrate the fact that money is only an idea. For example, there is never as much money in circulation as is transacted in business in a day. Suppose, for instance, I take a client to lunch and pay the restaurant fifty dollars. The restaurant owner uses the fifty dollars to pay a supplier for fresh vegetables and other foods. The supplier, in turn, uses the fifty dollars to pay a truck driver who delivers the food. The driver then buys food and clothing. Transactions totaling two hundred dollars take place rapidly using only the original fifty dollars. This illustration makes two points: first, the importance of cash is highly exaggerated, and second, *money is only an idea!*

Another related idea about money is that its value varies and depends upon *what* is bought, *when*, and *where*. A twenty dollar bill does not, of course, mysteriously change into a fifty or a hundred, but its value varies. In the hands of a foolish or extravagant spendthrift, a twenty dollar bill might purchase only five dollars' worth of goods. At a different time, in the hands of a discerning person, the twenty dollars might be used wisely to buy goods that can become worth fifty dollars. The Bible itself says that "wealth certainly makes itself wings" (Proverbs 23:5). Enjoying enduring wealth requires a watchful eye on purchases and investments because money is only as valuable as choices make it.

A familiar example of money's fluctuating value is merchants' willingness to sacrifice some profit through reduced sales prices. Willingness to alter the value they place on their inventory is influenced by their need to secure cash, to pay taxes, to get rid of existing inventory to make room for new items, or various other reasons. At such times, the consumers' dollar is worth more, but when shortages of some vital product cause prices to go up, the consumers' dollar purchases less.

The fluctuating value of money is only one of many variables I take into consideration when planning for my financial success. While the impulse buyer is not likely to become financially independent, I have learned by experience that neither is the overly cautious. Those who genuinely know money—with all its characteristic merits and foibles—and use it with judgment and daring gain the prize of financial success. These insightful individuals literally spend their way to wealth as they wisely invest and acquire assets that appreciate in value such as securities, real property, and equities. To those who understand money, these are just some of the ideas that money represents.

When people ask me how they, too, might enjoy the same financial success I have earned, I can almost feel my mother's hands on my head as her words echo in my memory: "You have everything you need right here between your ears..." First of all, I tell them, believe that you have unlimited potential for financial success and growth. Second, recognize that you are personally responsible for your financial achievements. Third, develop an attitude and belief that *money is only an idea.*

28

TAKING RISKS

Frankly, I have never thought much about taking risks. I believe risk taking is just something that entrepreneurs do naturally. Through experience they make better and better choices and decisions about when to take a risk.

About fifteen years ago I was in Acapulco with my friend Mark Haroldsen. His organization has probably conducted more seminars in the last fifteen years on how to invest in real estate than any other organization in the country. I remember sitting under a palm tree at the Pierre Marquez Hotel, doing some work, looking out at the ocean, and anticipating playing tennis that afternoon. Mark inquired, "What are you doing?" I answered, "I am writing an article, a speech, and a lesson for one of our programs—all built around the courage to succeed."

Mark asked to see some of my notes, so I shared them with him. He started laughing and said he needed to do a takeoff on my topic and write a book called *Courage to Be Rich*. I told him he was certainly welcome to any of my notes, and added, "I know there is a need for this." He responded, "If you only knew, P. J. Let me tell you a story."

My friend then told me about a seminar he was conducting for more than a thousand people. One day he just thought he would ask all the people who had been to his seminars before to raise their hands. He was startled at the large number who raised their hands. Then he asked how many had been to his seminars twice. And then three times. He reached up to five times, and more than a hundred people raised their hands.

Next Mark asked several to tell about some of their real estate investments—very few had even made any investments. He said he was startled that the people there had gained so much information about investing in real estate but had done so little with it. It dawned on him that you can get all the information and all the education in the world, but you have to get started. You have to take a chance. You have to believe in the fact that you can make the right selection, the right choice, the right decision, and you can make that first investment. You have to believe in yourself. You must take a risk!

This discussion went on for a while between us. Mark concluded, "P. J., I think the singular difference between you and all the other entrepreneurs I have known is that you take calculated risks. You think things through, you set goals, and you plan. But you also *take action*." And he is right.

I have met many people who have said, "I have tried that once and it didn't work. So I'm not going to do that again." I have a stock answer for people like that, "I once had a pair of pants that shrank, but I didn't quit wearing pants."

In other words, it is not what happens to you, but rather it is your *attitude* toward what happens to you. The old saying "nothing ventured, nothing gained" is literally true.

Study risks only briefly and you realize that getting out of bed in the morning is taking a risk. Driving your car is taking a risk. The chance of getting cancer from cigarette smoking is one in three. Your chance of death from a traffic accident is one in five thousand. Your chance of injury in the workplace is one in five thousand. Your chance of dying as a pedestrian is one in forty thousand.

So far as lifestyles, people actually live very happily with great risks because they have grown used to them. The Californians and Japanese, for example, live quite contently in their earthquake-prone cities while Sarajevans and Sri Lankans learn to step around bomb craters on their way to work. Perception has a great deal to do with it. People respond to images, not to probabilities. They react to what they visualize and what they imagine in their own minds about what is taking place.

Doing anything involves some risk—from financial loss to physical harm. Successful business people learn the art of "taking a calculated risk." I have also noticed over my lifetime that I learn from past mistakes and previous risks. My judgment is getting better. I think this comes from previous experience and maturity. I make fewer "wrong decisions" each day of my life.

My average success in predicting well what works and what will not gets better and better. I am currently in my sixties, and I would say that somewhere between 80 and 90 percent of the businesses I start now, or invest in, succeed. In my fifties, somewhere between 70 and 80 percent worked out. In my forties, only about 50 percent. In my twenties and thirties, somewhere between 20 and 50 percent of my ideas worked.

In my lifetime I have started or invested in over one hundred companies. The majority of those I started, and a few companies I bought into. Sixty-five percent of those I invested in did not work. Only 35 percent succeeded. This brings my lifetime batting average to something like 35 percent. I guess if you compare my success rate to baseball it is very good. One who bats .350 in baseball is in the top 1 percent of all batters.

During the past fifty years the biggest risk I have taken that turned into a fiasco, or "bust," was heavy investing in real estate in the late seventies and early eighties. During that time the tax benefits were tremendous and the depreciation was excellent. This all came to a screeching halt when the laws changed in the mid-1980s. Everybody was in the same boat; on a national scale many were left holding the proverbial sack—somewhere in the area of three hundred billion dollars in losses. My part of that was in excess of twenty-six million dollars. I thank God every day that I had the reserves—savings, earnings, and income—to survive that stormy time without going into debt to cover my losses. Hundreds of thousands of people in the United States were not so fortunate because they did not have any other reserves or any other resources; they took too big a risk with too much leverage and ended up in bankruptcy. Steve Bright, an attorney in Dallas, Texas, and also a very good friend, has represented me and my family for over twenty-five years. Steve says of me, "The only difference between Paul and most other people is his willingness to take a risk." Steve elaborates, however, that the risks I take are very well-thought-out, calculated risks, and not taken in a foolish manner.

I remember when I was an eighteen year old in the United States paratroopers. Getting into the plane was taking a risk. I knew that jumping was taking a risk. But I also know when I was jumping, I was stretching my capabilities. I was challenging myself. I had zero fear.

Jumping was a well-thought-out, calculated risk. I knew what I was doing and how to do it well. It was not foolhardy.

We were told what the statistics were and what the odds were—like a million to one you were safe when you followed instructions and did what you were told.

I did my best. I knew that being a paratrooper would be a growth experience.

A life without taking risks and a life without taking chances to me is a stagnant and stale existence.

One of the surprises in my life has been how little most people know about taking calculated risks. For instance, I have been asked to speak at business schools on entrepreneurship, and the students' responses have shocked me! Few of them knew what they were going to do with their education or their courses on entrepreneurship. In quizzing them, I learned that they were not equipped to take any risks. Students and others often are inhibited by the fear of committing themselves to action. To risk is to exceed one's usual limits in reaching for a goal. A certain amount of uncertainty is simply part of the process.

A great example of this is Kerri Strug, the 1996 Olympic gymnast who took a big risk on her final vault. She was under extreme pressure—the team's gold medal depended on her final score. On her first vault she had "messed up," at the same time injuring her ankle. She knew her ankle had been sprained. But after checking her strength and the possibility of continuing, she decided to *go for it*—to take the risk—and with a dogged determination she performed a beautiful vault. She won the gold for the team!

Taking a risk is loosening up on the *known* and the *certain* and the *safe* to reach out for something you are not *entirely* sure of but that, according to your best evaluation, will work. Risking is like jumping. Sometimes you *think* you know where you are going to land, but you are not always *certain.* We cannot grow by staying in our comfort zone. We cannot explore our potential and expand it without taking a risk or taking a chance. Whether you are going to get closer to another person or start a business, it is all a risk.

Many people do not want to take a risk until they know that everything is exactly perfect. They sit back and wait for the perfect moment, the perfect investment, the perfect situation. The trouble with that approach is that it almost never comes. Similarly, numerous people analyze and think about it too long—worry about it—they simply choose to *avoid all risks.* Successful people take chances. Successful people take risks.

Obviously a balance is essential between investigating and checking—studying and analyzing—and actually taking action. But a point comes with many opportunities when you lose more *by waiting* and *doing nothing* than you could possibly gain by additional checking.

Some people become addicted to taking scary, foolish risks because they get a euphoric "high" from the mere uncertainty of the risk. I am not talking about these foolhardy kinds of risks at all. Everyone knows that kind of risk taking results in self-destruction. I am talking about intelligently thought-out, calculated risks. I take a risk just by driving a car for example, but I am very cautious. I have driven an automobile for over fifty years and have never put a scratch on one. My father trained me to drive the most intelligent way to protect myself and those riding with me. So in that area of life I minimize the risks; I am a careful, responsible driver.

I have lived a lifetime of thinking, planning, and then jumping in—taking a chance—and it has paid off handsomely for me. People ask me about different businesses I have started and how I knew when I had enough information to make an investment in real estate or any other venture. I tell them I always ask myself some questions:

- What are my goals?
- Can I reach my goal without taking a risk?
- What are the benefits to gain if I take this chance?
- What can I lose by taking a chance—by risking?
- What can I do to prevent these losses?
- Is the potential loss I am thinking about greater than the possible gains?
- Is this the right time to take this action?

- What pressures are on me to make this decision?
- What would I have to know to change my mind about taking this risk?
- What experience do I have taking this type of risk?
- Who is someone I can confide in or ask for advice about this risk?
- Do I have personal blind spots in my vision about this risk?
- If I take this chance, this risk, will people think more of me or less of me if I succeed? Do I really care?
- If a loss does occur, will I take it personally, or am I able to be realistic and objective about it?
- Will I worry and worry about the risk I have taken?
- Who else has made a similar type of investment besides me?
- What actions can I take to track my investments and protect them?
- How will this risk affect me, my children, my parents, my friends, my company, my relationship with any bank or institution?
- Do I really enjoy the lifestyle of an entrepreneur?

Fortunately, anything that has ever happened to me in my role as a salesperson, a businessperson, an investor, has never affected who I am as a person or reduced my self-image. I have always just figured it was a risk I did not have sufficient knowledge about or that the timing was wrong. I chalked it up as experience that I could use for continuous growth as a person and as an entrepreneur. I make a conscious decision to manage my life to maintain a healthy self-image, peace of mind, and happiness.

I also feel very strongly that we need to accept personal responsibility for our lives—for the choices we make and the actions we take. Being taught to take responsibility for my decisions has helped me to think more, study more, analyze more. In addition, I rely on my spiritual beliefs to guide me and provide peace of mind about my decisions for taking certain risks. An especially powerful affirmation for me is Philippians 4:7-8: "Be anxious for nothing, but in everything by prayer and supplication, with thanksgiving, let your requests be made known to God. And the peace of God which surpasses all understanding will guard your hearts and minds through Jesus Christ."

I have to be totally honest about my personhood. My feelings must be unguarded at points. I must be vulnerable and open. I must exercise my freedom to be the very best person I can possibly be. I made the decision early in life not to be "a timid feeder in the lagoon." I have tried to live by the philosophy that you must take a risk if you want to sail out, head home, and fight the windswept foam with the cargoes of the world. It is not the gale but the set of the sail that determines which way you go. That is the choice of the navigator. I have always asked myself, "Am I the navigator of my life?"

What is the opposite of this? It is suffering from the paralysis of analysis and the fear of taking a chance, the fear of getting out of a comfort zone. I remember in the past twenty years since I took up playing tennis that I would go to the tennis club, and there would be so many people who never did anything but hit from the ball machine, or hit on the backboard, or practice serves. I never saw them play very much. I also like golf, and I have noticed I have a lot of friends who go to the driving range and hit, and hit, and hit. They never get beyond practicing. They never really play the game.

I have also observed there are some people who earn degree after degree. The university becomes a cocoon, a womblike

Taking calculated risks awakens something dormant in us. It paints in Technicolor on the canvas of life. It changes the film on the reels of life from black and white to full color. I took this picture of a double rainbow in Snowmass, Colorado, to remind myself that taking intelligent, well-thought-out risks results in the multicolor beauty of a rainbow.

existence in an academic arena where they feel safe and secure. No risk is involved, no chances are taken.

In selling, this *paralysis* or *fear* is referred to as "call reluctance." Salespeople either quit selling, make fewer calls, or stay in the office and rationalize because they are afraid people will strike back where it hurts most—at their desire to be loved, accepted, appreciated, and wanted. So they do not make the phone calls. They do not make the sales presentations. They fail because they fear taking a risk.

The real value of taking risks and moving into the unknown in any area is not how much money you are going to make or how big or how small the result. The most profound value lies in the fact that this decision is yours and that it gives your life deeper meaning and provides a wellspring of added strength. Identifying promising opportunities, studying them, and making sound decisions—taking calculated risks—makes you feel more alive and well-balanced, a Total Person!

29

LET'S MAKE A DEAL!

OVER THE YEARS I have made the majority of my income from commissions on sales and royalties received from writing courses (programs) sold around the world. I have invested these funds but in a nontraditional way, exposing a trait of mine—entrepreneurship. I have a lot of fun in business. I enjoy negotiating, the "thrill of the chase," making a deal. I am thankful I have never taken myself or the business world too seriously but consider it, rather, to be a lot of fun. This story is about some of the most unique deals I have made as an entrepreneur and ones I have enjoyed the most.

About fifteen years ago after church, I was reading the paper when I saw in the real estate section a small ad—very small—advertising an apartment complex in a city about a hundred miles away. I could not imagine an ad that small for such a large apartment complex. Out of curiosity I called. An eighty-five-year-old man answered the phone and told me he was selling the complex for a friend who was not well. I told him I was coming down in a private plane and arranged for him to meet me at the airport. The real reason for my having the gentleman meet me at the airport was that I did not want him at his house answering the phone when others called about the ad. I wanted to be the first one to see the complex. My instinct was quite correct. The complex was a good one at a good price. After I looked at it and we had negotiated over a cup of coffee, I asked him if he was authorized to make a deal. He said he was. Since neither one of us had a contract form, we took the paper place mat from the restaurant, turned it over, and wrote a contract on the back of it. I gave him five hundred dollars as a deposit with the agreement we would have my lawyer and his lawyer draw up a contract the next day.

While we were writing the contract, I found out that if the owner sold the property, he would have an enormous capital gains tax. I asked him, "What are you going to do with the money?" He answered, "I'll pay the tax and put the balance in the bank and live on it." Next, I asked him what his estate would do with the money when he died. The man's wife almost cried; she said she did not know why God had put them here with no children to leave it all to. I told them maybe He did give it to them so they could leave it to some children.

When I asked their religious denomination, they explained they were Southern Baptists. I said, "Why don't you give the complex to the Baptist Foundation for their Seminary?" Then I explained, "That money could be used to train many young people to be ministers, teachers, and other Christian workers. The Baptist Foundation would take care of you the rest of your life. You could live wherever you wanted to live, drive whatever kind of car you wanted to drive, do whatever you wanted to, in exchange for the apartment complex." They took my advice, and they donated the complex to the Baptist Foundation of Texas. Later I bought the apartment complex from the Baptist Foundation, kept it for some time, filled it with tenants, and made many upgrades and improvements. Within twelve months I sold the property and made half a million dollars profit. All this from answering a one-half inch ad!

A peculiar twist was that the owners were not going to give the eighty-five-year-old man a commission because the complex was a gift. At the last second, I told them I would kill the deal for them unless the elderly man received $25,000. He received that amount. It was a Godsend for him because of his age. We were close friends until he died.

I was in a building in Waco one time getting a shirt cleaned. The woman waiting on me had a foreign accent. When I asked her where she was from, she told me. When I asked what her husband did, she told me he was overseas. Next, I asked her if she was interested in selling her building. She said she was interested in selling it because she did not like living and working in that area. But she could not sell it until her husband returned, which would be in six months. She told me his arrival date, and I told her I would be at her business the morning after his arrival. I put the date on my calendar and showed up that morning six months later. I enjoyed a cup of coffee with the husband and wife and explored the possibility of their considering a trade for the building. I traded two houses for the equity in their building. I was happy, and I made two other people happy.

Another unusual real estate transaction I made took place about thirteen or fourteen years ago when a young man came to my house and told me he knew where approximately thirty duplexes would soon be for sale at a very low price. He knew they were going on the market and he would like to buy them, but did not have any money to make the purchase. He said he would give me the name of the person, take me to him, and introduce me to him if I would give him five thousand dollars.

This appeared to be a promising opportunity, so I agreed to go with him to meet the person. We agreed if I bought the duplexes I would give him five thousand dollars as an introduction fee. The young man was not in the real estate business and did not have a real estate license. The deal was made within three hours after I met the owner. We shook hands and wrote a contract on the back of an envelope with a one-thousand-dollar cash deposit. That is all the contract there was until we closed on this property at the title company. My family still owns these duplexes. They are performing very well, so it was an excellent investment.

Another quite unusual real estate transaction began when I received a call from an attorney friend in Dallas who told me about a farm near Belton and Salado that was being sold because the owner of the land was declaring bankruptcy. A half-dozen real estate agents would be meeting down there for a mini-auction; they were going to buy it and split it up into pieces.

The next day I went to the farm. It was in the late fall of 1986, and there was a light drizzle. The farm was completely trashed out. It certainly did not look like it was worth what they were asking except that Summers Mill was a famous landmark, and the river was magnificent. I had to use my imagination to visualize what could be done with the rest of the farm.

When I asked the owner what he would like to do, he answered that he would like to stay there on the farm. Next, I asked what would happen to him if the real estate agents bought it today. He answered that he would have to move. When I told him I would buy it right now and allow him to stay, he agreed to sell it to me. We wrote the agreement on the back of a three-by-five card. I gave him five hundred dollars cash as a down payment and bought it. He stayed for a year. It was a win-win situation!

I am thankful we own Summers Mill because many people have enjoyed it so much. We have kept it as a premier tourist attraction. I have been told that it is the most photographed place in the state of Texas.

Summers Mill has since been used for business meetings and conventions. People from all over the world have been there. It has been used for ministries—men's and women's retreats, couples' retreats, and Bible studies.

Since buying the farm, I have bought fourteen contiguous farms to put together a very unique combination—a thoroughbred horse farm on one side of the road and the Chisholm Trail Wild Bunch Ostrich Farm on the other side of the road. Both farms are doing very well. Recently my granddaughter, Jessica Meyer, had her thirteenth birthday party there. Her schoolmates told her it was the best party of the year. They played tennis, volleyball, basketball, threw horseshoes, played board games, rode paddleboats, and had a barbecue. In short, they had a lot of fun!

On another occasion, I was taking a tennis lesson at the Lakeway World of Tennis from the number one player in the world in my age group. During the lesson, I noticed a lot of condominiums nearby. I asked how many there were. My instructor said there were about a hundred of them altogether. I asked about a row of condominiums that looked empty. The tennis instructor explained they had not been selling well and that about twenty of them were still empty. When I asked how long they had been empty, he answered, "Two years." When I asked who owned them, he said "The Hunt family in Dallas." When I asked him who was in charge of them, he said their attorney was. He gave me the attorney's name but said it would be foolish to buy these condominiums because the market was suppressed and they had been selling very slowly.

Of course, I could not wait until the tennis lesson was over. I immediately called the attorney in Dallas. I guess he thought I was crazy because I said I would buy all twenty of them if he would finance them. Crazy or not, he said he would be glad to finance them, and we closed the deal in about thirty days. I started renting the condominiums and putting them up for sale. Because I love tennis, we went there about every two weeks for two or three days to play tennis. I began to sell the condominiums, one at a time, to people on vacation I met there. I would walk around the tennis courts and say to individuals, "I remember when I was doing what you are doing and wished I owned one of these condominiums you are renting now." I told them I would show them how they could own one. Over five years of going down there, playing tennis, and meeting people, I have made more than one million dollars' profit on those condos.

Even more important than the money I made was the fun and relaxation my family enjoyed there; it was one of the favorite places for our family to go for vacation because it is located less than one hundred miles from Waco. In addition, I sold condos to several friends who still enjoy them. I am thankful I had a tennis lesson that day. I am thankful I observed what was around me. I am thankful I asked questions and had that initiative to take action.

The stories in this article are just a small sampling of the fun-filled negotiations I've enjoyed over my lifetime. The thrill of the chase and the words "Let's make a deal!" supercharge my entrepreneurial enthusiasm. Recently one of my children said, "Dad plays Monopoly with *real* buildings and land!"

30

MAXIMIZING MY STRENGTHS

PETE FOUNTAIN has enjoyed renown as a world-famous clarinet player. Not only have I enjoyed listening to him play the clarinet, but I also like him as a person. I got to know him when I bought his 1936 four-door convertible. Several years ago, our World Convention was held in New Orleans, Fountain's hometown. Coincidentally, our convention theme that year focused on maximizing strengths, and Fountain just happens to be one of the most impressive examples of maximizing strengths I have ever known.

When Pete Fountain was still a young teenager, he began to play the clarinet. Almost immediately he knew he had found his strength. His teachers, however, told him not to bring his clarinet to school. They said he needed to join an athletic team and have fun like other boys. But he refused to listen. He knew he was not a boy who played the clarinet—he was *a clarinet player!* Fountain invested all his energy in his music and became the number one jazz clarinetist of his time. Pete Fountain maximized his strengths!

A popular myth says we can do anything if we put our mind to it. That sounds inspiring and a bit noble, but it simply is not true. Physical limitations, for example, keep many people from doing some things they might like to do. I know some very short, thin people who like football, but it is obvious that no matter what they do, they can never play on a professional football team. Take me, for another example. I love football, but considering my age, height, and weight, you can imagine what would happen if I were hit by a lineman on any of today's teams. I would be carried out on a stretcher!

In our self-improvement business, we teach people about the amazing power of desire and motivation. But we also teach them to be realistic and discerning about our different gifts and strengths. When people ask me what accounts for my success in life, I point out how I have concentrated on my strengths instead of my weaknesses—my potential, propensities, and possibilities instead of perplexities and problems. I bask in the sunshine in my life as much as I possibly can, rather than hiding from the dark, the clouds, and the rain.

Special wisdom may be required to discern the personality traits that enable us to do one thing or prevent us from doing something else. An abundant amount of desire and motivation can compensate for certain personality tendencies. But I have noticed over my lifetime there are some firmly established personality traits that simply will never change. I have often said, for example, that I am not the personality type who would enjoy preparing accounting reports. If I had to spend most of my day analyzing figures and producing reports, I would soon cease to function effectively. I avoid tasks that use my weaknesses. Instead, I hire accountants and keep myself free to exuberantly pursue opportunities and responsibilities that maximize my strengths.

My mother, a schoolteacher, taught me early in life the wisdom of maximizing my strengths. One of the stories she shared with me as a young person illustrates the advantages of learning how to use strengths and manage weaknesses. A group of animals, she explained, decided to have a school so they could all become well-rounded and successful. The students included a duck, a fish, an eagle, an owl, a squirrel, and a rabbit. They all made suggestions about what they should study and settled on five subjects—running, swimming, tree climbing, jumping, and flying. The first day of school began with running class. The rabbit excelled. He was so excited he could hardly contain himself. "I love school!" he said. "We do what I do best." The teacher encouraged and praised him and promised him that with practice he would become a champion.

The squirrel was average in running and came in second, but all the rest of the animals failed. The next class was swimming. The rabbit did not really want to go into the water, but the teacher insisted. "You may not like it now," the teacher explained, "but five years from now, you will know it was good for you." The poor rabbit jumped in and quickly went under and would have drowned had the other animals not pulled him out. They all laughed at the poor wet creature who resembled a rat more than a rabbit. When report cards came out, every animal received at least one high grade, but they were all so poor in most other subjects that they earned low grade point averages.

The wise old owl was the only one who realized it was the school itself that was failing—not the students. The owl said, "We should have schools where we are allowed to concentrate on what we do well—where some animals could run all day, squirrels would be allowed to climb trees, ducks and eagles could fly, and fish could do nothing but swim." This story may seem simplistic, but unfortunately, many otherwise intelligent people simplistically try to become well-rounded to the extent that they are much like a fish trying to learn to fly.

I am the beneficiary of an incredible heritage. My mother and father gave me a fortune when they conditioned me in a positive, creative way. I started my first self-improvement company because I realized that a majority of people were not as lucky as I had been but were victims of negative conditioning. They were programmed to fall short of using their potential. Conditioned to fail, the only way these countless individuals could reprogram themselves was to throw their conditioning out the window and concentrate on their strengths instead of their weaknesses.

Thoreau, an early American essayist best known for his attacks on the ineffective practices of social institutions, insisted that people must use their strengths even when they are different from the strengths of most other people. He said individuals often called nonconformists are those who possess the invincible courage to "march to a different drummer."

"Woulds," "shoulds," "musts," "oughts," and "do it my way" or "my way is the only way" are all expressions of the emasculating philosophy dictating that everyone should follow a certain pattern. Many parents, for example, are obsessed with the idea that their children must go to a particular college, perhaps because they went to that college or because that college is prestigious. In Waco, for example, a forceful pressure exists in our community for young people to attend Baylor University, known all over the world for its excellence. But I am convinced some students would be better off attending the excellent two-year college in our community or our outstanding technical school. In addition, some parents almost insist on their children's pursuing a certain career without study and analysis of their strengths.

People have frequently asked me how I have known what my strengths are. I tell them it is a process of self-evaluation. I determine where I stand at the time as a result of using my strengths. I look closely at the potential I received at birth, my personality type, my creativity, my ability to form relationships with other people, what gives me the greatest sense of fulfillment and happiness, and how I can make the greatest contribution. I feel even more strongly today than ever that the quest for identifying, evaluating, and using my strengths has been well worth the effort.

> I feel even more strongly today than ever that the quest for identifying, evaluating, and using my strengths has been well worth the effort.

One of the foremost indications I am using a strength is experiencing a sense of excitement about developing and using it. Even if putting the strength to use requires work, it is not drudgery. I have fun using it! I love to write, for example, and enjoy each stage of developing a new program. The sense of excitement I experience is obvious evidence that when I am writing, I am operating out of a strength. Another example relates to salespeople. Many individuals in sales have told me they enjoy a feeling of exuberance when making a sales presentation to a client. Quite the opposite, people who do not like sales work fear it, can never get it right, are sapped and drained at the end of the day, and are probably operating out of a weakness. A career in sales is not an intelligent choice for those people, and they should consider pursuing some other career.

Another benchmark I have used to determine my strengths is the magnitude of my motivation to use and develop those strengths and abilities. Even though they may have been undeveloped at the time, my way of thinking about them convinced me they offered possibility and I was eager to work on them. I knew early in my life that my strengths were in the areas of people skills, persuasive skills, selling, and entrepreneurial activities like starting businesses. That was what I liked to think about and where my motivation and desire increased as I developed these skills.

In contrast, one of the greatest horrors of my life occurred when my father took me to a foundry to explore the possibility of working there and pursuing a career. I had never been in a foundry where they make patterns and cast objects in metal. It was dark, smelly, and noisy, and I felt absolutely zero interest in it. My instinct, my gut reaction, everything within my inner being knew, "This is not a place for Paul J. Meyer. This is not where I want to be!" I also knew it was a place where Paul J. Meyer was *never* going to be.

Another evidence of using one of my strengths was how quickly and easily I learned a skill or activity. When I improved steadily with anticipation of getting better quickly, I was confident I was operating out of a strength. I remember a youth named Orville Gonzales. He moved to my hometown from one of the islands in the Pacific with his dad, who traveled and worked on army posts. At first, Orville would come out and watch us play basketball. Orville had never dribbled a ball in his life—he had never even had a ball in his hands. But within thirty days after he started playing, he was outshooting all of us who had spent several years practicing. Orville simply had a gift for it, an eye for it, a hand for it, the depth perception, and an instinctive understanding of how the angles of the backboard worked.

Orville was, in contrast, a klutz with a tennis racket—awkward, clumsy, uncoordinated. After two or three days of giving it his best, he concluded, "I don't think this is my game. Even more important, I am not interested in it, have no desire to learn it, and I am not going to pursue it." Orville saw very quickly that the old rule "practice makes perfect" was not working with his tennis, whereas it had worked with basketball. Orville was a classic example of one who was a master at minimizing his weaknesses and maximizing his strengths.

When I consistently performed with excellence over a period of time, I also knew I was operating out of one of my strengths. I knew, for instance, when I started selling, it was an almost inborn strength. I love to sell. It is a joy for me. It is simple. It is easy. I am highly productive, effective, and efficient when I am selling. Over time, I have not grown tired or bored with selling. Selling is obviously one of my strengths.

Another clear indication I am operating out of a strength is feeling positive and confident and having a good self-image when engaging in an activity requiring that strength. I guard against overgeneralizing because I recognize that when we begin a new skill, we do not usually feel 100 percent positive about it. If we are operating out of a strength, however, after a small amount of experimentation and trial and error, we can sense fairly accurately whether this is something we are going to feel good about doing. I have always kept a related factor in mind. People with low self-esteem imagine they have only weaknesses. So they fail to recognize their strengths but spend their time worrying about improving their weaknesses. They could improve their effectiveness and their self-image if they would put their weaknesses on the back burner and concentrate on their strengths. Because this strategy enhances a positive self-image and maximizes productivity, I have persistently applied it in my own life.

When I am operating out of one of my strengths, the activity regenerates me and creates additional energy. Practicing this strength motivates me and reinforces an already positive self-image. Some years ago, a reporter asked the coach of a Chinese Ping-Pong team how the team practiced. The coach said they spent at least eight hours every day practicing their strengths. They found this type of practice developed their strengths to the maximum and that their strengths compensated for their weaknesses. He gave a further example of one of the players' hitting every ball with a forehand. The player did not have a good backhand, so he just used his forehand so efficiently he could not be beaten. This simple illustration is a great reminder to apply the same principle of maximizing strengths in every area of life.

"I am *stressed out* if not *burned out*," a business associate told me several years ago. "I am glad you have admitted your plight to me," I told the associate. I continued, "I often wondered why you had chosen that line of work. I think it is simply not based on your strengths as I have observed them." This man immediately pursued other career opportunities and is now happily working in a job that minimizes his weaknesses but maximizes his strengths. I see absolutely no evidence of his former complaints of being stressed out or burned out.

How does this apply to me? When I grow disinterested in certain entrepreneurial pursuits, I simply change directions to something that does engage me, motivate me, and bring out the best in me. Or I delegate. Delegating has been one of the greatest boons to my being able to maximize my strengths. I delegate responsibilities or tasks I am not particularly good at or do not have any interest in. An example in my personal life is handiwork around the house—that is one arena I simply do not like. I do not want to use my energy on doing something that takes away from tasks and responsibilities I am genuinely interested in and good at. An example in the career area of my life is paperwork. I do not like to do it, so I delegate most of it. Delegating frees me to pursue activities that I enjoy and that have a high payoff.

I am doing what I do well and love doing—writing! I am dictating the final touches on this story, "Maximizing My Strengths."

The crucible test of using my strengths is reviewing my successes. Keeping a list of my successes and reviewing it tells me at a glance what works best for me. When I hit tough times—as all people do from time to time—I do not dwell on the weaknesses or the bad times. Instead, I do a mental 180-degree turn to remember past successes and past pleasures. Reliving the thrill of my accomplishments reminds me to rivet my attention on what I do best so I can maximize my strengths.

"The mass of men lead lives of quiet desperation," observed Thoreau. Decades ago, when I first read his writings, I made a conscious decision and a conscious commitment never to fall under the umbrella of that observation.

I have kept this commitment.

How?

By minimizing my weaknesses and *maximizing my strengths*.

31

BROKEN TRUST

MANY PEOPLE have difficulty trusting others. I have never had this problem—I love people. I do not see them as they are now; I see them as who they could become if they used more of their God-given potential. I see them living fulfilled lives, and I do not mind being open or vulnerable as anyone certainly is when trusting someone.

In families, children trust parents and spouses trust one another. In business, banks trust company officers who sign notes to see that the notes are repaid, and people are given positions of authority and are trusted to fill those places responsibly. Stockholders and owners of the world's businesses delegate authority for operations to people in positions of trust.

So it is a sad day for anyone who loves, cares, and trusts another to have that trust broken. In the Meyer Family Enterprise group of companies there are over forty businesses that operate internationally. With a wide breadth of locations geographically and a wide diversification of types of businesses, we must necessarily rely on selecting people we can trust for positions of leadership to run these companies.

Several times in my business career I have experienced the pain of broken trust—the disappointment that people have failed to act with integrity in their business dealings with me.

The first such major experience I had came when I was still a young man. I had joined an insurance company domiciled in Georgia and accepted the opportunity to be the agent for all of the company's sales in the state of Florida. I quickly went to work to demonstrate my ability to carry out the job I had been entrusted to do. Over a period of a year, I recruited a large sales force, trained them, and began to generate a large volume of business.

Unknown to me, the Insurance Commission of the State of Florida called upon the company to increase its capital funds in the state to cover the large amount of insurance my agency had been selling. Instead of complying with this directive, the president of the company had mismanaged the company reserves and had taken the money produced from sales in Florida out of the state. One Monday morning I arrived at the office to find the building completely empty. Over the weekend several big trucks had been backed up to the office. Everything was loaded and carried to Georgia. Desks, files, office equipment—everything was gone. A quick phone call revealed that the majority of the bank accounts were also gone.

I was initially devastated by what I felt was a personal betrayal but quickly realized that I had several hundred insurance salespeople working for me who were out of a job—just as I was. I also knew that the people who had bought policies from our agency could lose their investments. I could not in good conscience fail all those people as the company's officers had failed me. My friend and partner Bill Armor and I worked for over a year to settle all the affairs of the company. We made sure our policyholders were protected and helped every salesperson in the agency find a new job. When everything was done, I had nothing left except the knowledge that I had done what was right even though others had not.

That was my first experience with broken trust, but not my last. In the early years after I established SMI, one of our young distributors quickly built a large sales organization and soon became the number one distributor in our organization that sells personal development courses. We worked with him, trained him, worked with his associates, and supported him as he built his business. Everything seemed to be going well. Then one day we discovered that he had ceased being our distributor and had become our competitor. He had produced courses paralleling every SMI program. His programs even quoted long passages from ours and had numerous other passages slightly reworded.

To protect our own product and our legitimate distributors, we were forced to sue the young man for copyright violation. The court recognized the plagiarism and ruled in our favor. This man eventually spent time in prison as a result of these and other misdeeds.

On another occasion, we had a person in a foreign country who had represented us and sold our products for twenty-five years. We had been personal friends, had enjoyed each other's company, and had been on several family vacations together. While representing us, he was also developing programs similar to each of ours. For some time after this was brought to my attention, I could not believe that this long-standing and trusted friend had broken the trust I had placed in him. We filed several lawsuits against him, but then I realized that he was past seventy years of age and had a number of health problems; so I dropped the suits because I still had a personal affection for him.

He also posed little threat to other people who depended on our business. If he had, I may have had to pursue legal action against him even though I cared deeply for him personally. I realized again that when there is broken trust, there is always pain.

On another occasion, one of our company officers—a personal friend—was in charge of our international business and traveled many times to Central and South America. I was shocked one day to find out that he was writing contracts with our associates in Latin America with one set of figures in the copies he filed here in the company and a different set of figures on the copies he gave to the associates.

The discrepancy came to light when one of the associates visited the Waco office. As we talked, I mentioned his investment of ten thousand dollars in the business, and he immediately said, "No, twenty thousand dollars." I thought there must be some mistake, but he produced his copy of the contract, we compared it with our file copy, and sure enough, they were different. We discovered that our company's officer was charging double, turning in half of the money, and taking the rest for himself in jewelry. He had a good credit rating, a good reputation, and a thoroughly likable personality; but unfortunately, the temptation was too much for him to resist.

Another experience of broken trust began when I met a young man in the late 1960s who had become a distributor for us. He was ambitious and hard working. He excelled in selling and in managing—a typical career-path high achiever. He soon accepted a management position in our home office. We became personal friends; we took vacations together; he was a person with a great deal of talent and personal charisma. Over a decade or so we made some investments together, and finally I came to like and trust him so much that I promoted him to CEO—and not of one company, but of a group of related companies. As an indication of how much I trusted him, I even named him in my will as the executor of my estate. I think that says it all.

Jane and I have spent approximately five months each year outside the United States for more than fifteen years. For several years, we took a tutor for our youngest daughter, Leslie, to help her with schoolwork. My trusted executive came on an occasional visit, and I clearly remember his saying on several occasions, "Trust me, Paul. I'll build you a large and profitable company."

Then one day it all collapsed. I received one of the worst phone calls of my entire life. The auditors had been working on the annual audit and called me to say, "All is not what it appears to be. What they have been telling you is what could be labeled 'managed information'—a little twist here, a little twist there, a bending of a fact here, a bending of a fact there, a stall here, a stall there." It was obvious that my trusted friend and associate had not lived up to my trust in him.

My first reaction was, "It's not so; it's not possible. I have total faith and confidence in him, total trust." But the answer came back from the auditors, from one of the people on the conference call, "I'm sorry to be the one to tell you: he has obviously broken your trust." I felt a strange, heavy lump of disbelief and disheartenment burgeoning inside of me. Further details provided by the auditors proved that he could not have done it by himself. Someone in accounting had to be helping because the books just did not add up. The skullduggery going on to cover-up-until-it-could-be-straightened-out was an inside job. I was stunned. The facts slowly sunk in though, as day after day, week after week, for several months, new details surfaced.

This broken trust hurt as much or more than anything that has ever happened to me in my life. It was more than the fact that soon our finances were in shambles with the debris of the destruction strewn everywhere. Most of all I hurt because I loved and trusted the one responsible, and I saw what had taken me the major part of my adult life to build being shifted from a rock-solid foundation into sand. Words cannot describe the depth of disappointment and disillusionment resulting from that broken trust.

A long, long time has passed since that incident, and it has taken millions of dollars to straighten it out and make it right. Many people were hurt, including about two hundred who lost their jobs. Even now the surviving companies remain much smaller than before.

We now have a new paradigm and a new system in place to prevent something like this from happening again. As a result of this experience, we have protected all our companies, the family, and myself from a similar future disaster. We have taken the accounting function from all the companies, and the executives of all our companies answer to a trustee group. We have checks and balances inside and outside the companies. This allows executives freedom to operate while giving them a structure for demonstrating their honesty and integrity.

Amazingly, what I am still most concerned about to this day is the loss of my friend who seems to have lost control of his life—no discipline, no boundaries. He seems to have crossed the line somewhere. I remember asking him after this debacle, "Why?" He replied simply, "Desperate people do desperate things." But he also said he was sorry he had disappointed me. Now *that* I believe. I still pray every day for my friend and his family. And oh yes, I forgave him a long time ago. I still add a "P.S." to my prayer wishing him Godspeed and the achievement of whatever dreams and aspirations he has and that some way, somehow, he will commit himself to achieve that without hurting anyone else.

Fortunately, my experience has been filled with many more people who have acted with integrity and have merited my trust than these few who have broken it. I still am willing to trust people, to believe in them, in spite of the hurt I have experienced when some have betrayed me.

You cannot glue hundreds of pieces of glass together and create a Waterford that once was.

How do I feel about these people who have been guilty of broken trust? I love them still. Thank God, I have learned to separate the person from the deed. I no longer enjoy a personal association with people who have broken my trust because it is too painful. But what is done is done—it is over. I harbor no bitterness and no animosity. But the close relationship can never be restored . . .

For me and for all those who were involved in these experiences, I believe that "today is the first day of the rest of our lives." We can each go our own way with a prayer that God has forgiven us all for our shortcomings and our failures and that we will all have another chance in another situation in which integrity will be the order of the day.

32

NEGATIVE CAPABILITY

I WAS OVER fifty years old before I heard the term "negative capability." I possessed the quality personally but had never identified it by that label.

A fabulously successful Singapore businessman, Y. Y. Wong, is the first person I ever heard applying this term to the business world. Mr. Wong, a billionaire, operates a group of companies all over Asia whose products are concentrated in seven areas: business machines, computer systems, consumer electronics, telecommunications, lithographic and graphic communication products, financial services, and engineering and technology. Mr. Wong told me that in the context of business, negative capability is the ability to bounce back from failure by overcoming obstacles.

Mr. Wong also said that he had learned everything he knew about *success* from his *failures*. He did this by analyzing why he failed and then by turning the negatives of failure into positives for success. He wasted no time in worry, doubt, or frustration over why he was facing obstacles. I found as we talked that Mr.

Wong's experience had closely paralleled my own. For him and for me, achieving success has been influenced largely by the ability to ignore the negative forces in the environment and to refuse to allow them to control today's and tomorrow's actions.

The English poet John Keats originated the term "negative capability" and defined it as the condition in which "individuals are capable of being in uncertainties, mysteries, doubts, without any *irritable* reaching after fact and reason."

Examples are everywhere of people who have used negative capability:

- Barbara Walters lisped when she first began her career. Yet by studying words and working hard, she has made her mark as an outstanding broadcast journalist.
- Though a quadriplegic confined to a wheelchair after a tragic diving accident, Joni Eareckson Tada paints, writes, and travels the world over, challenging people to consider their positives or strengths and not their weaknesses.
- Jim Abbott, the famous baseball pitcher, rests his glove on the nub of his right hand, delivers the pitch—at ninety miles per hour—and quickly switches the glove to his left hand. With only one hand, Abbott does not think of himself as disabled. He uses negative capability: he concentrates on what he can do—not on what he cannot do.

I have held fast to the attitude that failure is final only if I quit trying. Giving up after a mistake or failure steals the opportunity for success in the future. Instead of despairing, I ask myself these questions: Why did I fail? What can I learn from this experience? How can I avoid making the same mistake again? With this approach, mistakes and failure can be transformed into stepping stones to success.

No matter how strong my positive mental attitude might be and no matter how carefully I choose friends and associates from positive, enthusiastic people, I am realistic and realize there will come times when I must deal with negative people. For example, when I was released from military service and felt ready to make my mark in life, I decided I wanted to sell insurance. After a number of rejections, I was finally hired by one company and told to ride with several other salespeople to a sales meeting. In the car I listened and tried to learn all I could from what the experienced people said.

With negative capability I earned membership in the insurance industry's prestigious Million Dollar Round Table—the youngest member who had ever been inducted into that organization.

Imagine my surprise when we reached our destination only to be told that I was fired. "You're too shy and not outgoing enough to sell insurance" was the reason given. I wanted to say that I was listening so I could learn—but the boss would not listen. Fortunately, I did not believe his estimate of what I was capable of doing.

The road to victory was not smooth. One month I made one hundred presentations without a single sale. A critic told me I evidently was not cut out to sell insurance. But I replied, "I'm going to make it next month." And I did. The next month was the best I had ever had, and the best the company had ever had. It happened because I refused to be "irritable" about the obstacles I faced.

Negative capability has enabled me to face unanticipated obstacles, to hear discouraging opinions and advice, and to meet failure—and still stay on track to achieve my goal. The quality of negative capability is most effective when I have a clearly developed set of goals and a written plan of action for achieving those goals. A carefully prepared plan of action has provided a firm foundation for dealing with whatever might happen.

Negative capability helps me deal with adversity above the level of emotional reaction:

- Instead of acting with irritability, I demonstrate calmness.
- Instead of exploding with frustration, I am filled with exhilaration.
- Instead of suffering as a victim, I conquer adversity with abundant energy.
- Instead of wasting time and effort wondering why I face an obstacle, I proceed to do what needs to be done next.

Another important aspect of negative capability—an absolute necessity for success—is the freedom to take calculated risks. Not every venture succeeds. Not every goal is easily reached. In fact, if no plan ever fails, that would be a sure sign that I am so conservative that I have not stretched to reach a new plateau of success.

In one sense, all of life is based on taking risks. Taking a risk can be reckless and foolhardy. I never take that kind of risk. Instead, my risk taking is the result of a carefully planned strategy with a sound basis for expecting success.

Several years ago I spoke to a group of college students who were part of an entrepreneurship program at their university. They wanted to know what characteristics were important to success for one who wanted to be an independent business owner. I told them that one of the most important traits they could develop was the ability to take calculated risks and to learn from the failures that would obviously result from some of those risks. I made a list of all the ventures I had entered that had failed. I was surprised myself to find that I have been involved in more businesses that proved to be failures than in those that have succeeded.

The raw number of failures is unimportant. What is important is that I learned from each of those failures. Instead of complaining about the unfairness of circumstances or sinking into despair, I studied my actions to discover what had gone wrong. Then I incorporated the principles I learned from studying the failure into my planned actions for later ventures. As a result, my successes—although fewer in number than my failures—have been far greater in total achievement.

> In every adversity is the seed of equivalent—or greater—benefit if you believe it, if you look for it, and if you work for it.

Negative capability enables me to assume a genuine sense of positive expectancy. When I remain calm and in control in the midst of negative circumstances, it is possible for me to believe in a bright future—to expect success in reaching challenging goals. Negative capability and positive expectancy make it possible to dream ever larger dreams, to attempt greater projects, and to enjoy enhanced success. Negative capability reinforces my long-standing belief that in every adversity is the seed of equivalent—or greater—benefit if you believe it, if you look for it, and if you work for it.

33

THE MOST AMAZING PERSON I HAVE EVER KNOWN

THE PHONE VIBRATED in my hand as the energy from the personality and voice at the other end came over the line. My friend and former pastor, Dr. Bill Hinson, had not exaggerated when he told me this person I had just called was an intense, vibrant, magnanimous individual. "You two are much alike," Bill said. He added, "You should get to know him." I was intrigued by what Bill had told me so I called John Edmund Haggai.

I have remained in awe of this astonishing individual ever since that first phone call. Over the next few years John Edmund Haggai and I talked frequently by long-distance telephone and corresponded, but crushing career demands prevented our meeting in person until the early 1970s. My wife Jane and I were walking through the Hilton Hotel near the San Francisco Airport when I heard someone speaking to a group of people in a meeting room. "That's John Haggai!" I told Jane. "I'd know his voice anywhere." When John's meeting was finished, I introduced myself. We immediately cemented the friendship already begun and began weaving the intricate and multifaceted tapestry of a lifelong friendship.

One word strikes me as I contemplate the intensity and the multiplicity of John Edmund Haggai's personality and sphere of influence in all that he does. That word is *amazing*. Since founding my flagship self-improvement and personal development company in 1960, I have been fortunate to associate with incredible individuals from numerous countries all over the world. In the course of my various business activities and travel, I have met dignitaries and other individuals singled out and set apart from all the others by their unique accomplishments and leadership skills. When I recall all the intriguing people I have ever known, John Edmund Haggai stands out as the most amazing among them all.

In addition to the one word *amazing*, I can think of a few other words that at least partially describe John. I say partially because it is impossible to capture the fullness of John Edmund Haggai with one word, one sentence, one paragraph, or even one hundred pages. But these words or phrases come to mind when I think of him:

- "This one thing I do..."
- Courage
- Focus
- Determination
- Concentration
- Persistence
- Zeal
- Passion
- Commitment

- Steadfastness
- Conviction
- Boldness

John's genuine interest in people and love for them is one of his many remarkable qualities. His concern for people is constant, consistent, and conspicuous. Once when we were traveling together on an international flight, he looked up at a flight attendant, called her by name, and asked about various members of her family. I was surprised because this was the first time this particular flight attendant had walked by us. After John finished the congenial conversation and the flight attendant proceeded with her duties, I asked him, "Who is this person?" John looked equally surprised at my curious question; he replied, "She is a flight attendant I met on this same flight about a year ago."

I soon discovered that John Haggai's fabulous memory for names and faces is demonstrated everywhere he goes. And John goes a lot! He made his seventy-ninth around-the-world trip in September 1996. John's extensive travel requires a great deal of time not only in airplanes but also in hotels and restaurants. No matter what weighty problem he faces or what urgent matters require his intervention, every individual he meets receives his genuine attention. John is equally at home with heads of state and other prestigious dignitaries. His love for people knows no social, geographical, age, or gender boundaries. John Haggai has friends he calls by first names from every walk of life all over the world.

John's consummate use of language is also amazing. He is a master communicator, whether he is talking one-on-one, to a small group at dinner, to a trustee meeting, to heads of state, or to an exceedingly large audience anywhere in the world. As a young man he was fascinated with words and how they fit together to express ideas and emotions. Once after hearing him deliver a masterful presentation to a group of high-ranking officials in China, I asked him, "John, how in the world did you ever learn to use just the right word and to explain complex ideas and make them so crisp and crystal clear?" He answered me in his characteristic crispness and clearness, "I worked at it."

John's writing skills are equally astounding. He has written many, many books on a wide variety of topics, and all profoundly affect the lives of countless readers because he expresses himself brilliantly in both the logical and emotional realms. John bases his books on sound doctrine and time-proven principles, and his stirring real-life accounts of actual people bring to life the points he makes. Here are some of the widely circulated titles from John Edmund Haggai's pen:

How to Win Over Worry (a bestseller since 1959 and published in fifteen languages)

How to Win Over Fear

How to Win Over Pain

How to Win Over Loneliness

Be Careful What You Call Impossible

My Son Johnny

The Leading Edge

Lead On!

The Steward

The Wachersberg Connection

Paul J. Meyer and the Art of Giving

I have read every one of John's books and savored each one of them. In addition, I have read almost every book on leadership ever published, but John Haggai's book on leadership—*Lead On!*—is one of the most profound, thought-provoking treatments of true leadership I have ever read. Another one of my favorites is *Be Careful What You Call Impossible* because John so frequently and faithfully does the impossible. More than anyone else I have ever known, John Haggai lives what he writes about. His books are monuments to what he believes, and he lives his convictions—a memorable example of Shakespeare's "Action is eloquence."

The book requiring John's gallant courage to write was *My Son Johnny*, the story of John and Chris's only child, seriously brain damaged by a negligent doctor too inebriated to respond as he should have to a difficult birth. This book has given other parents hope that they, too, could go on living after such a tragedy. That was John's expressed purpose of writing the book, that it could be used by God to comfort and encourage other parents who also suffer. Telling this heart-wrenching story and sharing his most vulnerable thoughts reveal John's amazing mind that reaches the heights of intelligence and his heart that has suffered the hurt only a parent who has lost a child knows. The last lines in the book about Johnny capture John Haggai's uncanny capacity for a wide range of emotions, from heartbreaking loneliness to earnest gratitude to God: "I miss him. Terribly, sometimes. But Johnny is free, free at last, and like his mother, I thank God."

John Edmund Haggai is an eternal optimist. He has many times faced opposition, crushing financial needs, and pressing personal frustrations, none greater than seeing his only child beautifully endowed with thoughts and dreams and the ability to pray fervently and effectively to God but unable to communicate with people and interact with them. John's faith, dignity, and spirit of hope have never been daunted. His positive attitude about life and the future is so contagious that everyone around him invariably feels its effect.

Throughout John's career, Chris, a merry-eyed blonde with a ready smile, has walked a quiet but supportive step behind her husband. I vividly remember strolling with this gracious Virginia-born lady, my wife Jane, and a few other people along the Great Wall of China. The people enjoying the continuity of history in this awesome setting were walking rather informally in small groups. John was with a fun-filled group a few steps ahead of us. We were talking to Chris about how it felt to be married to a person with such a powerful personality as that of John Edmund Haggai. In all of John's manifestations, Chris said in so many words, he was simply the most exciting thing that had ever happened to her. "Whenever John joins a group," Chris said in her soft Southern-belle voice as she glanced his way, "it's like a party!"

John Haggai's supercharged energy also has never ceased to amaze me. Although he is now past seventy years of age, he still puts in what would be for most people a long, grueling day of work—every day. John plans his schedule and carries it out with the utmost of adherence to complete all the projects he plans. He arises early every morning for a time of prayer and Bible study. He includes regular exercise, faithfully working out on an Airdyne bike, and has logged thousands of miles on it. He also gives careful attention to a healthful diet. He and I have both been through the world-famous Cooper Clinic in Dallas, Texas. Once I asked John's physician about his impressive health, hoping the doctor might share with me the source of John's boundless energy and other secrets that John obviously had found at Ponce de Leòn's mythical Fountain of Youth. The doctor looked at me, smiled wryly, shook his head slowly, and said simply,

John is amazing.

John's gregarious nature and all his other amazing attributes put him head and shoulders above others. For instance, he maintains a voluminous correspondence and makes hundreds of telephone calls every week from wherever he happens to be in the world at that time. Eager to take advantage of time-saving communications technology, he has become adept at using a laptop computer. Whenever he meets a new person, he takes time the same day to write a letter to that person and transmits it to the computer in the home office so it can go out in the mail the next day.

When you survey John's filled-to-overflowing calendar and his astonishing accomplishments, you would conclude he does not have time for a hobby. Not so! He has enjoyed a lifelong love affair with automobiles. As a child, he could recognize every model of car on the road and knew something about each one. He has nurtured that interest, and it makes its appearance in the most unexpected situations, often with John's uncanny sense of humor. For example, he met an executive several years ago who had just joined one of my companies. A 1965 Ford Mustang was in the parking lot near the building where she worked, and John assumed—correctly—that car belonged to that executive. After dispensing quickly with business matters with the executive, he asked the usual questions car buffs ask and, of course, relished every morsel of exchanged information. Several years later, when John was in Waco, Texas, he delivered the morning message at the same church that executive attended. Looking out across the audience as John spoke, he recognized the executive. Within moments he found a place in his sermon, much to the amusement and delight of the audience, to ask her if she still had that 1965 Mustang.

International travel might well also be a hobby of John Haggai's because he does it frequently and effortlessly—it seems to serve as a wellspring of energy and rejuvenation. With the next around-the-world trip to be his eightieth, John is a veteran traveler. Such long flights crossing several time zones leaves many travelers with jet lag. Not John Edmund Haggai! He never seems to suffer from that complaint. Wanting desperately to follow his example, one of my executives who travels extensively once asked him for advice. John replied, "I've learned to drop instantly to sleep while traveling. I refuse to worry about problems or challenges facing me at my destination." John added, "I also plan carefully to make sure I eat the right foods and not too much, so that *my body* and *my brain* will function when I get to where I am going."

John Edmund Haggai is the most disciplined person I have ever known. The discipline and focus required to drop off to sleep instantly on an airplane is only one of the countless examples because John demonstrates that same focus in all that he does. John's ability to focus is manifested most magnificently in his career, avocation, and his life's mission, as carried out by the Haggai Institute for Advanced Leadership Training. This unique organization trains Christian leaders from Third World countries in effective methods for evangelizing their own people. This incredible mission is the result of John's focus and passion to make the Gospel of Jesus Christ available to people in Third World countries. To date over twenty-three thousand trained leaders are working effectively in 142 different countries to make a difference in the lives of their people—differences that no "outsider" has ever been able to orchestrate, regardless of training. It would probably be safe to say that John Edmund Haggai knows more about foreign missions than anyone else living today.

While many outsiders are looked upon with disdain and cynicism, John is revered with respect and appreciation because he provides training to individuals recognized as leaders in their own country. Dorcas Bola Adu, Ph.D., of Ilorin University in Ilorin, Nigeria, attended a Haggai Institute leadership session in the early 1980s. Since that time she and Albert, her Nigerian husband, have served as Christian and civic leaders in Ilorin. Dr. Adu voiced the heartfelt opinion of many people from Third World countries around the globe when she said, "We love John Haggai. He is a wise man."

John Haggai's interest in the Third World countries began in earliest childhood. John's father was born in Syria and fled to the United States to escape religious persecution in that country. His father's stories about life in the Middle East gave John a sense of kinship with that part of the world; that kinship was reinforced every time he looked into a mirror and saw his face that looks so typically Middle Eastern. The Haggai name and John's personal appearance have enhanced his ability to develop rapport with church and government officials in many parts of the world. But the respect given him is more than a matter of looks or a name; John demonstrates genuine empathy for people no matter where they live. John Edmund Haggai is also the most astute world citizen I have ever met or known.

That's my friend, John Edmund Haggai —the most amazing person I have ever known.

John Haggai can best be described as a modern-day Apostle Paul. His passion and his commitment to a single purpose give him a compelling charisma unmatched in anyone else I have ever known. When I read what the Apostle Paul writes in his letters to the Philippians, those words ring in my ears in the full, rich voice of John Haggai:

> *But this one thing I do, forgetting those things which are behind, and reaching forth unto those things which are before, I press toward the mark for the prize of the high calling of God in Christ Jesus.*
>
> Philippians 3:13–14

That Scripture describes John Edmund Haggai perfectly. He never looks back with regret, with pride, or with excuses. He enjoys the present fully, but he also looks to the future with faithful anticipation.

34

"BIG EARS" PAY OFF

THE FIRST TIME anyone ever mentioned that I had big ears was the day I was born in San Mateo, California. My father's sister lived in San Francisco just north of San Mateo, and she came to the hospital to see her new nephew. She made a casual comment that I had very big ears for the size of my head. This offended my father, but it has never bothered me.

Learning to use my "big ears" to listen effectively has brought me numerous—and profitable—exciting experiences. I am fully convinced that "big ears" pay off! Once when I was a young salesman, for example, I enjoyed my first big financial windfall from using my "big ears." I was in a country store one hot August day drinking an RC Cola and eating a fried pie. The store was quite small—only three or four tables—and I overheard a conversation at another table. Two men were talking about some nearby land for sale that could be bought simply by paying the overdue taxes. I listened carefully, got into my Commodore Hudson automobile, drove into town, and asked where I could get some more information about this land.

As a result, I bought three lots. Next, I enlisted a friend to join me in a venture to make a profit on these lots. He built three small homes on them, each around eight hundred square feet, with cement floors, cement block walls, pine cabinets, and no paint. We sold these homes for $4,500 and made $1,500 profit on each one. That was quite a bit of money at that time so my "big ears" paid off handsomely. I decided I would learn to listen to all sorts of odd bits of information to see whether I might use some of it.

I am thankful I have a built-in radar system with big ears and the mental alertness to go with them.

In about 1952 or 1953, I was in a restaurant on the top floor of the Columbus Hotel on Biscayne Boulevard in Miami. I was having lunch with a man and trying to sell him a life insurance policy. I overheard J. Paul Riddle, the founder of the forerunner to American Airlines, pleading with Arthur Vining Davis to help his company, a cargo airline that was in serious financial trouble. More than eighty years of age at that time, Davis was the retired chairman of the board and cofounder of the Aluminum Company of America. He finally consented to lend Riddle several million dollars. When they reached across the table and shook hands, J. Paul Riddle said, "You are an angel."

I told my prospect I had to go to the restroom because I was not feeling well. I took the elevator down twelve floors to the Francis I. DuPont securities firm on the ground floor. I went in and told the broker I wanted to buy one hundred thousand shares of Riddle Airlines at forty cents a share. He asked if I had ever bought stocks before, and I said, "No." He asked me if I knew that the company was in trouble, and I said, "No." I bought the stock for forty thousand dollars—money that I did not have—rushed back upstairs, and completed my insurance sale. After lunch, I called my friend Bill Armor, and we went to several banks. Finally one of Bill's friends loaned me the forty thousand dollars largely on the basis of his respect for Bill and their friendship. In a little over six months, the stock went up to over five dollars per share.

I decided to sell, but the broker told me that if I dumped that much stock on the market all at once, the stock would go down to two dollars. So I went to the Arthur Vining Davis estate, sat by the gate, and waited until he came home in his limousine. His security people stopped me, but Davis asked what I wanted. I told him I had some stock that no one would buy. He took me into his den, and I told him exactly how I got it. He said, "That's a great story, young man. You will do well in life." He bought the stock from me, and I made my half-million-dollar profit.

On another occasion I was in the lobby of a savings and loan association filling out a deposit slip when I overheard two men talking. One of them said, "I need to sell this apartment complex immediately since the loan is due, and I am not going to get anything for my equity if I don't do something." I politely interrupted and asked, "I couldn't help but overhear your conversation. Where is the complex?" He said it was located about sixty-five miles from Waco. I told the man I would like to take a look at it. He agreed, so I immediately stopped what I was doing and went to look at the property. We made a deal and shook hands without a contract. I got a loan, and we closed on the deal in one week before the end of the month when he needed it completed. I kept the property twelve months, then sold it to some people in California and made six hundred thousand dollars on it.

Another time I was having lunch in a restaurant and overheard two people talking. I asked, "If this is something you're not interested in, can you tell me about it?" They told me about an exceptionally good deal on some land. I bought the land for $250,000 and immediately put it back up for sale and made one hundred thousand dollars' profit on it.

I have learned over a lifetime some very, very important principles about listening:

1. Never talk confidential business in a restaurant or any other public place.
2. Keep your ears open in public places and listen for opportunities. Be alert; be observant; pay attention; see and hear what others miss; create your own luck.

I have also enjoyed some benefits from others whose "big ears" helped me. The wife of an executive in one of our companies was in a restaurant and overheard two attorneys talking about suing a friend of mine. They discussed the tactics they planned to use to win the case in court. The executive's wife went home and told her husband, he called me, and we alerted my friend to the plan. My friend used the information to save himself a great deal of money.

Another time, a department head in one of our companies mentioned casually to a group of friends at church that he was looking for an assistant. One of the men in the group owned an employment agency. A few days later he found a client who seemed to meet the qualifications for the job. He called and arranged an interview. The woman we hired as a result of that casual conversation eventually became the president of one of our companies and worked with me for over twenty years.

I do not believe in being underhanded or in sneaking around to learn about other people's business or in using information I hear to damage anyone else. But I appreciate any scrap of information I hear that I can use creatively. It is within this context I have found that "big ears" pay off!

35

MY FAVORITE THINGS

IN THE DELIGHTFUL movie *The Sound of Music*, Maria sang the song, "My Favorite Things." Because the items she names reveal something of her personality and attitude, her list nudged me to consider "What are my favorite things?" Here are some of *my* favorite things:

- My favorite pastime is talking to people. I agree with Goethe, considered one of the greatest thinkers of all time, when he said, "Conversation is the most sublime of human activities."
- My favorite color is red, traditionally recognized as the color for courage.
- My favorite character trait is integrity.
- My favorite person is my wife Jane.
- My favorite new car is the Lexus.
- My favorite old car is the 1936 Ford Cabriolet.

- My favorite sport was basketball as a youth, and now it is tennis.
- My favorite spectator sport is a toss-up among baseball, basketball, and football.
- My favorite exercise is riding a bike.
- My favorite inspirational cassette is Jonathan Livingston Seagull.
- My favorite book is the Bible.
- My favorite movie is the original Stagecoach.
- My favorite religious song is "How Great Thou Art."
- My favorite popular song is "More." (It is also Jane's favorite.) Here are some of the lyrics:

> *More than the greatest love the world has known,*
> *This is the love I give to you alone.*
> *More than the simple words I try to say,*
> *I only live to love you more each day.*

- My favorite interview is one conducted more than twenty years ago by Mitsuko Shimomura, considered one of the top female journalists in the world at that time.
- My favorite airplane is the Lear 55.
- My favorite plane to pilot is a fifty-year-old Piper Cub.
- My favorite vacation spots are first, the Cayman Islands; second, Palm Springs, California; and third, Aspen, Colorado.
- My favorite language to listen to is Spanish.
- My favorite number is thirteen. The most important reason—my first son, Jim, was born on March 13.

- My favorite food is rice.
- My favorite dessert is chocolate-vanilla swirl yogurt.
- My favorite novel is Charles Dickens's A Tale of Two Cities, especially its first line, "It was the best of times, it was the worst of times …" (It all depends on attitude!)
- My favorite poem is "High Flight."
- My favorite time in life is right now.
- My favorite saying is Carpe Diem! (Seize the Day!)

36

KNOWLEDGE IS POWER

A FRIEND, STEVE BRIGHT, AND I were recently discussing what it takes to be successful. We talked at length, agreeing upon the absolute necessity of a positive, "can do" attitude. Steve then said something that startled me, "Paul, you have not succeeded in your professional endeavors just because of your positive attitude." He continued, "Your phenomenal success can also be attributed to your *knowledge*." Steve's belief that I minimized the power of knowledge seemed ridiculous to me. To the contrary!

From my earliest days I have fully recognized and respected the truism "Knowledge is power," first spoken by Francis Bacon in the late 1500s. I have consistently contended that knowledge is essential for success regardless of the nature of one's career—CEO, manager, entrepreneur, or any other pursuit.

As a teenager, I also remember my dad advising me, "Never take a position without first being an apprentice."

What was he really saying? As I gained experience and business expertise, I comprehended more fully the wisdom of my father's well-founded advice. Over the years I have observed that the most effective individuals know their business inside and outside, from bottom to top. Several people in the fast-food industry are classic examples. Consider Dave Thomas, founder of Wendy's. He started out as a dishwasher in Annapolis. A similar story can be told about Herb Cain. He admired the president of Pillsbury, Win Wallin, and asked him for advice. Wallin's advice was similar to my father's; Wallin recommended, "If you want to run a business, start at the bottom and learn it from the ground up." Cain followed that advice and is now chairman of the board, CEO, and part-owner of Godfather's Pizza, a serious competitor with other large pizza chains. Both Thomas and Cain began as apprentices, so to speak, with positive attitudes and determination to gain knowledge about business from bottom to top. The success of Thomas and Cain, like that of many other outstanding individuals, verifies the saying I have heard many times through the years: "You can't tell what you don't know any more than you can come back from where you've never been."

Another observation I have made about knowledge is that the more I know about a business opportunity, the stronger my desire grows and the more motivated I am to work toward the achievement of my goals for this particular opportunity. Or in contrast, I have found that after acquiring more knowledge about an opportunity, if my desire and motivation do not also increase, this particular opportunity may not be right for me. Perhaps it would not maximize my strengths or does not appeal to my interests. In this way, knowledge provides a crucible test for desire. Gaining knowledge gives me a firm basis for making a decision about whether or not I want to pursue a certain opportunity.

Even if I am still quite interested in an opportunity, if I do not increase my knowledge substantially, my desire is simply not sustained. In other words, a small amount of knowledge will not sustain desire or motivation. Once I have decided—on the basis of a certain amount of knowledge—that I want to continue pursuing a possibility, then acquiring more knowledge always fans the flame of my desire.

My experience has also been that knowledge provides a wellspring of satisfaction. Learning about topics of interest to me has always been a source of fulfillment whether for work or for play. I collect 1936 Fords. To increase my fun and satisfaction, I have read extensively about Henry Ford's life. I have read numerous books on the history of the automobile industry and joined an automobile collectors' organization. I have read all of the books and manuals I can find on restoring antique cars, especially Fords. I network with others who share this interest to learn as much as I can from them. Over a ten-year period, I have become very knowledgeable about '36 Fords and other antique cars. I am not a neophyte. I know a "stock" car from a "restorod" car from a "street rod." And antiques are just my hobby! I get even more satisfaction and fulfillment learning all I can about the various businesses I own.

No doubt about it—knowledge also increases my confidence! I know from experience that my knowledge bolsters my confidence. When I know what I am talking about, I can pursue my goal enthusiastically because self-confidence gives me a clear vision of my goal and creates desire that is strong enough to sweep away almost any obstacles. One of my lifelong interests, for example, is marketing. I have read every book I can get my hands on regarding this topic. I have subscribed to every marketing newsletter on this topic, and I have searched out information on it wherever I can find it. People who are proving their expertise in this area are rich sources of information. I enjoy talking to people and exchanging ideas with them. I have found that it is true in any arena of expertise that high performers generally have an "abundance attitude" and are eager to share their know-how as well as their enthusiasm.

Another fine distinction I have observed is that knowledge is more than just the acquisition of facts; knowledge is a source of an inner quality of assurance that ignorance simply cannot match. Knowledge is the mental backbone that holds firm while ignorance is flabby and uncertain.

A CPA and university professor who is a friend of mine is another good example of this. He recently received the most prestigious award given by the school of business at the university where he teaches and conducts research. First of all, he was required to acquire extensive knowledge to qualify as a certified public accountant. To maintain this professional certificate, he is required to participate in extensive continuing professional courses every year. He does just that—and then some. He reads every book and every article he can find related to his area of teaching and research expertise. He networks with like-minded professionals. If there is a seminar anywhere that will add to his knowledge, he attends it. The fact that he learns as much as possible about accounting has enabled him to perform expertly in that arena.

My oldest son, Jim, is another excellent example of this success principle. Jim enjoys a well-earned reputation as an outstanding attorney. Over the last twenty or so years, I have seen him do just as my accountant friend. Jim reads, studies, goes to seminars, and networks with other outstanding attorneys. Jim always works hard to be on the cutting edge of his profession. My friend and my son know that *knowledge is power!*

Comprehensive knowledge offers another benefit: It has helped me make fewer mistakes than most other people. For instance, I have pursued with a vengeance information about capitalism, entrepreneurship, and related topics. In addition, I have also studied the opposite philosophies and concepts—communism and socialism. I have studied the strengths and weaknesses of each of them; I have analyzed what each can do and cannot do. I am convinced that my extensive knowledge has kept any mistakes I might make to a minimum.

I have also seen how comprehensive knowledge has enabled my son Larry to make fewer mistakes. The scope of knowledge Larry gathers when considering a business opportunity is phenomenal. He does his due diligence more completely than anyone else I have ever known. Larry's business experiences and my own make it clear to me why I have such a rigorous dedication to preparation. To put it in the words I usually use to express this idea, "Prior preparation prevents poor performance."

My friend Steve and I continued discussing the concept that *knowledge is power* over several months' time. In one of these thought-provoking conversations, he made an accurate observation: "We live in an information explosion, an era called the Information Age." He then asked an excellent question, "Paul, how do you get a grip on all of the information or knowledge you need to successfully pursue all your business interests?" I took his question seriously because I firmly believe in this success formula:

POSITIVE ATTITUDE + KNOWLEDGE = SUCCESS

Here is how I broke down the process to answer my friend's question:

1. **I identify common knowledge.** Before I invest in any business, I read everything I can get my hands on about it. I ask the experts questions. I listen a lot! I make it a point

to know all the ins and outs of the business—and certainly more than the competitors know.

2. **I acquire new knowledge**. After learning the basic knowledge that everyone else knows about a company, industry, product, or service, I search diligently for new knowledge. Knowledge is everywhere in this era of the information superhighway—the Internet, CD-ROMs, seminars and workshops, books and manuals, business publications, newsletters, the business sections of large reputable newspapers, and the list goes on and on.

   I read somewhere that people have to earn the equivalent of a college degree every seven years just to keep up with all of the technological changes. I believe this is

Taking advantage of modern technology—with a little help from her mother, Janna—my granddaughter Morgan is learning at an early age that acquiring knowledge is fun.

true. Furthermore, I also contend that there is no excuse for failure to acquire new knowledge when so many opportunities for acquiring new knowledge exist. Attending the three-month course at Purdue, for example, is just one example of the many seminars I have attended over the years.

3. **I create new knowledge**. After studying information from all the various sources, I think about it, analyze it, extract the best concepts from it, combine the best ideas from different sources, and create a new slant or innovative ways to provide improved products and services.

   My ability to analyze information and relate the normally unrelated has served me well. Years ago, for instance, when I saw that my employees simply were not comprehending information I was giving them, much less using it, I began summarizing the salient points and recording them on the reel-to-reel recorders. At the time this was a novel approach; no one else was doing it, and it proved fantastically effective.

   Later I purchased a small portable player from England. I adapted the player for use in the car so that busy people, whose time was at a premium, could listen to the tapes while driving. I have been told I was the first person ever to do this and that I am the father of this industry. I simply saw a need and figured out an innovative, highly effective way to meet it.

4. **I lead and manage people who work with knowledge**. I consistently share knowledge with the people in all of my corporations. I have given away enough books to fill the Library of Congress! I consistently make it a practice to

encourage people to learn, to share, and to explore possible ways to do their jobs better. I view all of my businesses as cauldrons of knowledge. My experience has proven over and over again that people, when encouraged to do so, come up with rich new ideas for improving effectiveness and productivity.

Solomon, considered to be the wisest man of all time, recorded in Proverbs 10:14, "Wise men store up knowledge."

Solomon's statement was sound and solid then, and it is a basic success principle for men and women today. It has been true in my own life, and I have observed it in the lives of many others—when the dynamic essentials of positive attitude and knowledge are combined, they energize actions and propel to the greatest heights of achievement. I have found it is literally true—knowledge is power!

37

SCHOOL OF HARD KNOCKS

THOUSANDS OF PEOPLE over the years have asked me, "Where did you go to school?" I simply tell them, "The School of Hard Knocks." I also tell them I love the school I attended because the campus has no boundaries. It is out on the highways and byways of America and all around the world. It is in the cities, and it is in the rural areas.

This school requires no preregistration, no deposit, no qualifying exam, and no entrance interview. This school is available to anyone who wants to attend, is willing to actively participate, and is serious about learning lessons for living.

I am especially grateful for all the students I have met in my many classes at the School of Hard Knocks. Every race on earth is represented—the students come from everywhere. They also come in every size, shape, and age you can imagine. They are both male and female. This special school maximized the advantages of diversity long before anyone ever heard of quotas or affirmative action.

The breadth of courses and the depth of the subject matter are incredibly impressive. More classes are offered than in

Harvard, Yale, Oxford, the Sorbonne, or the University of Tokyo, or other great institutions of higher learning.

Another feature I like about the School of Hard Knocks is that the best students never graduate! The most effective learners continue their education at this alma mater for a lifetime.

"Black and blue" are the well-earned colors of my school. They come from the bruises and hard knocks that diligent students receive from participating in the rigorous curricula.

My children and grandchildren are curious about our school cheer. I tell them it is all about "Ouch!" This is the one word I learned to say when knocked down, criticized, or attacked by others. Refusing to stay down, I repeat the cheer and then get up and enter the game of life even more enthusiastically than before.

There are no short courses, no quick fixes, and no free lunches. The professors do not hand out education in tablet form for students to swallow quickly and be on their way along the road to success. And they do not give education in a prechewed and predigested pabulum. I learned to bite off a lot, and I learned to chew a lot. I had to work to absorb it and to apply it.

In the School of Hard Knocks, I have learned some incredible attitudes and principles for success that have served me well for a lifetime:

1. **SEIZE THE DAY!** Those courses teaching this success principle have been the most fun! I have loved learning to develop a seize-the-day attitude—staying alert, being a good listener, having my radar out for every opportunity to meet people and to expand my horizons. I have spent many hours of trial and error learning in the laboratory of life to turn theory into practice—to dream new dreams and set higher goals.

The words of William Shakespeare remind me of the importance of a seize-the-day attitude: "There is a tide in the affairs of men, which, taken at the flood, leads on to fortune; omitted, all the voyage of their life is bound in shallows and miseries." I have learned to seize the day by seeing the potential in other people and encouraging them to use it. I have learned to seize the day with a loving heart and a forgiving spirit. I have learned to seize the day to help as many people as I can in as many ways as I can and in as many places as I can for as long as I can.

2. **TAKE PERSONAL RESPONSIBILITY.** What I have learned about responsibility in the School of Hard Knocks has not been confined to the classroom; it applies to every area, attitude, and action of my life. It is one of the most useful courses—one I recommend for everyone. When you accept personal responsibility for your life, the whole world looks different. When you know it is up to you, you prepare better, study more, learn more, and have greater resolve.

When you accept personal responsibility for your life, you also learn to use more of your God-given talents. People who accept personal responsibility take more initiative and show more self-reliance. Since there are fewer and fewer people who are willing to take personal responsibility, you stand out. When you learn to accept personal responsibility, you are recognized as a leader and more opportunities for advancement come your way.

Schools of higher learning require studying the classics. One nugget of wisdom I remember from Plato summarizes responsibility: "Take charge of your life. With it, you can do what you will."

3. **THINK OUTSIDE THE SQUARE.** Learning to set my imagination free, to be creative, inventive, and resourceful, and to think beyond the obvious was another exciting course that has served me well. Teachers always have a list of terms for their students to memorize, and I remember an excellent definition of creativity: "*Creativity is looking at what everyone else looks at but seeing what no one else sees.*"

   Being creative involves these capabilities and attitudes:

   - Relating the normally unrelated.
   - Seeing potential and possibilities others never see.
   - Seeing stepping stones where others see stumbling blocks.
   - Seeing possibilities where others see problems.
   - Seeing solutions where others are blinded by insurmountable circumstances.

   These nontraditional, innovative ways of looking at the world have helped me create the ideas for each and every business I have started over the past forty years. The idea for my brother's first fiberglass business came from relating the normally unrelated. The idea to start my first company almost forty years ago, Success Motivation Institute, and put condensed information on LPs came from seeing potential and possibilities that others did not see. The money I have made in real estate has come from seeing what other people could not. I learned early in my life that real intelligence is the creative use of knowledge—not merely the accumulation of facts.

Thinking outside the square was fairly easy to me as an adult because my parents taught me the basics when I was young. For instance, once when I was with my dad shopping in San Jose, California, we went into a model shop where model airplanes were sold. I wanted to buy a model airplane, but my dad said, "No. Design your own." I did not know anything about building model airplanes. After a "healthy discussion" with my father, he agreed I could buy one airplane so I could learn how to build one. But the next one I had to design myself; I had to buy the raw materials and build it on my own.

Using my mind to think outside the square helped me become more imaginative, inventive, and creative than my counterparts and has been both personally satisfying and professionally profitable.

Words cannot describe my heartfelt satisfaction when I completed, after one year of work, a personally-designed, six-foot wingspan, gasoline-powered airplane.

4. **NEVER, NEVER, NEVER GIVE UP.** I have learned through this school that in every arena—every phone call I make, every letter I write, every business deal I consider—never to give mental recognition to the possibility of defeat. This approach provides me with an invincible attitude that I *can* and I *will.*

   If life is easy for a person, with few or no changes or challenges, that person must be coasting downhill, taking the course of least resistance. Although this was one of the most difficult principles to learn, I saw others demonstrate it again and again—the downhill road requires minimum effort and leads nowhere special. People have to work and push to make anything go uphill. The trail to the mountain top, the pathway to the stars, demands work and persistence.

   I have learned that 90 percent of all failure comes from quitting too soon; so hanging on with persistence has given me the best possible chance of reaching my goals. Nothing in the world can take the place of determination; talent will not, genius will not, education will not. Hanging on until success comes is the essence of determination and persistence. Many lessons of determination are demonstrated in nature:

   Drops of water falling three or four times a minute
   eventually wear a hole in a granite boulder.

   The constant force of the wind twists
   a giant tree into a shape entirely
   different from its nature.

   My all-time favorite quote about determination and persistance comes from Winston Churchill. He spoke these memorable words at a crucial turning point of World War II,

> Never give in, never give in, never, never, never, never—in nothing, great or small, large or petty—never give in except to convictions of honor and good sense.

5. **HONESTY PAYS OFF.** "Honesty is the best policy" was instilled in me as a way of life by my parents. If any prerequisite was required to succeed in the School of Hard Knocks, this was it. I learned early that life is made up of our choices. The doors we decide to open or close each day direct our lives and determine our destiny. The impact of even the smallest decisions we make is captured by these lines:

Sow a thought, reap a habit.
Sow a habit, reap a character.
Sow a character, reap a destiny.

Using honesty and integrity as my basis for every decision has also helped me guard against the fatal habit of not making decisions when they need to be made. If people will not decide, then in effect they have already decided because, as William James, the great psychologist, put it, "When you have to make a choice and don't make it, that in itself is a choice."

I recently read an article in the *Wall Street Journal* pointing out what I learned long ago in the School of Hard Knocks. The article reported that a consultant firm asked numerous top executives to cite the primary factor in their success. Integrity was consistently given as one of the top five reasons for personal and business success.

My father and mother would both be proud that I have earned a good grade in this course; what they taught me has lasted throughout my lifetime.

6. **LIVE LIFE PASSIONATELY**. Learning to live life fully and savoring each moment of it is one of the most satisfying aspects of the School of Hard Knocks. Theodore Roosevelt, the twenty-sixth president of the United States and a Nobel Peace Prize winner, offered a challenge I have incorporated into my own philosophy of living life passionately: "*Far better is it to dare mighty things, to win glorious triumphs, even though checkered by failure, than to take rank with those poor spirits who neither enjoy much nor suffer much, because they live in the gray twilight that knows neither victory nor defeat.*"

My affirmation for living life passionately is Psalm 118:24: "This is the day the Lord hath made; I will rejoice and be glad in it."

I have learned to live my own song because when I am singing my own song it comes from my heart. I have studied the lyrics, the harmony, and the melody. I simply do not see how people can sing a song they have not lived. People without passion, with no zeal for living, are only a dormant force, only a possibility, like an immobile stone waiting for the blow of the iron to give forth sparks.

Living life passionately requires continuing education based on the premise that nothing grows unless it is green, and anything that is fully grown is ripe and will soon rot. Living life passionately fuels the fire, the desire, the dynamic motivation behind every worthwhile purpose and the joyous pursuit of simply being alive.

In the graduate course of living life passionately, I learned to avoid worrying. Instead, I climb more mountains, walk on more beaches, watch more sunsets, cry when something touches my heart, and laugh when something tickles my funny bone.

My affirmation for living life passionately is Psalm 118:24: "This is the day the Lord hath made; I will rejoice and be glad in it."

7. **LIVE WITH A SERVANT'S HEART.** In the School of Hard Knocks people are given awards, trophies, and other types of recognition for outstanding contributions of one kind or another. The most prestigious awards, I have observed, go to those who render service to others. That is the way it should be. As for me, I do not measure success by how high I climb but by how many people I bring with me. I measure my success by how well I motivate people to use their full potential.

   The top professors in the School of Hard Knocks seem to agree that the greatest leaders are those who serve others:

   - Ghandi said, "You will find yourself by losing yourself in service to other people, your country, and your God."

- Socrates said, "All people have one goal—success or happiness. The only way to achieve true success or happiness is to express yourself completely in service."
- Albert Schweitzer said, "I do not know what your destiny will be, but one thing I know, the only ones among you who will be really happy are those who will have sought and found how to serve."
- The Scriptures say that the one who will be greatest among you will be servant of all.

THE FINAL EXAM. When I started out as a serious student in the School of Hard Knocks, I was mostly raw material. But as I worked my way through the courses, every knock enhanced my understanding and helped me grow wiser, and every knock opened a door to a greater possibility. I have learned first-hand the truth in the Russian proverb that says, "The same hammer that shatters the glass forges the steel."

I have also learned to appreciate more fully the striking symbolism in the fact that a diamond and a chunk of coal are, in the beginning, the same. The difference is in the final result. The diamond has gone to the School of Hard Knocks; it has been subjected to long and intense pressure to make it indestructible, beautiful, and more valuable than a chunk of coal. In my seventh decade of life, hopefully a little bit of diamond is beginning to glimmer through. I feel somewhat more like a diamond, but I know I will need polishing for the rest of my life.

The stories I have shared in this book illustrate *what* I have learned and *how* I have learned it. I have earnestly tried to live out what I have learned. Incorporating the lessons of life into my everyday attitudes and actions has been the key to whatever success I have achieved.

Thank you, Mom and Dad, for the magnificent fortune I have inherited—having your genes, living in your home, and being exposed to your thinking, teaching, training, and attitude. I renew my promise to you that I will pass this inheritance on as best I can to my children, to their children, to my friends and colleagues, to my clients, and to everyone who crosses my path for as long as I live.